A

I0390602

Birder's

Collection

by RJ & IrisBenjamina
Chris Johnson Nature Photography
Copyright 2019. All rights reserved.

Book 1

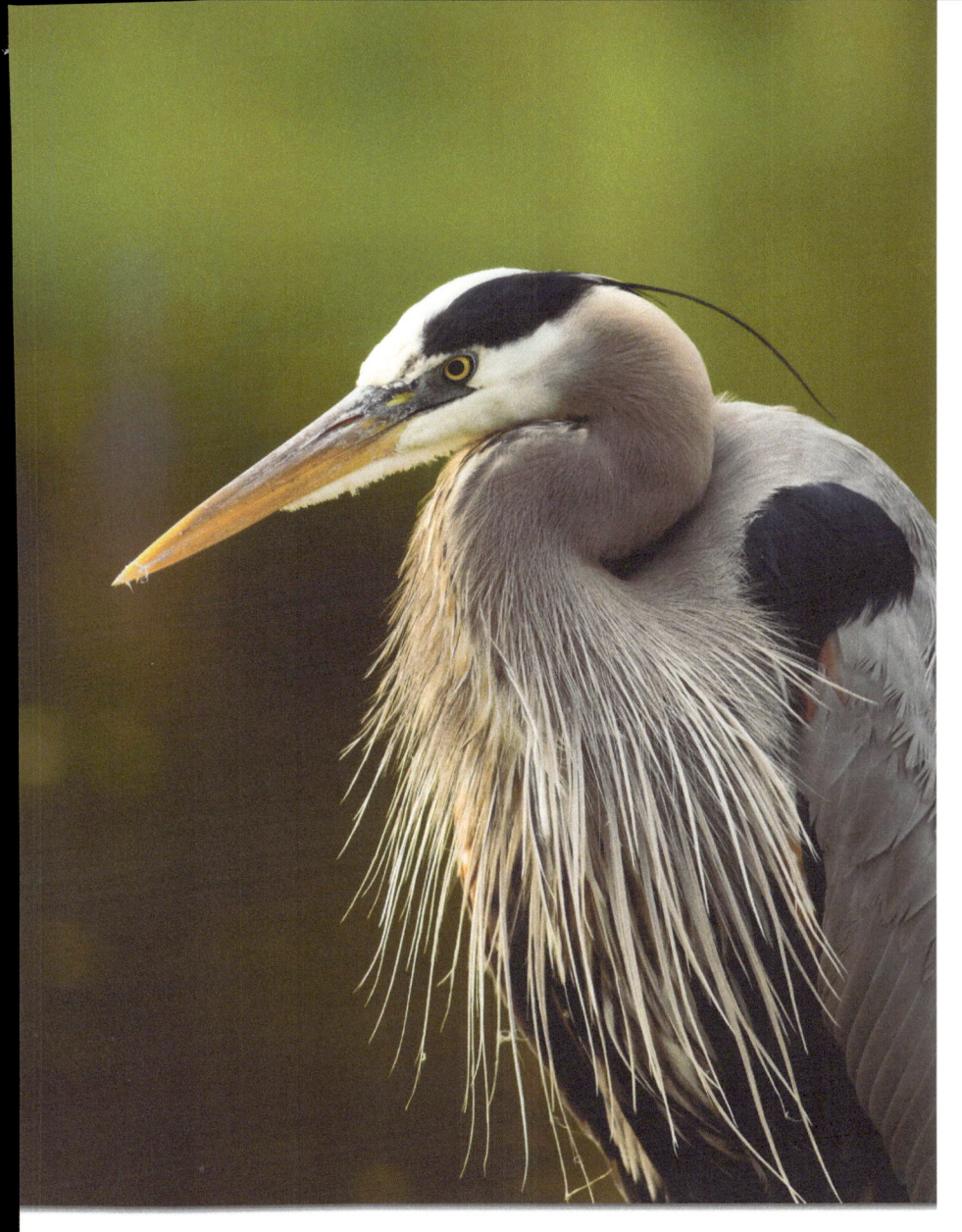

Great Blue Heron

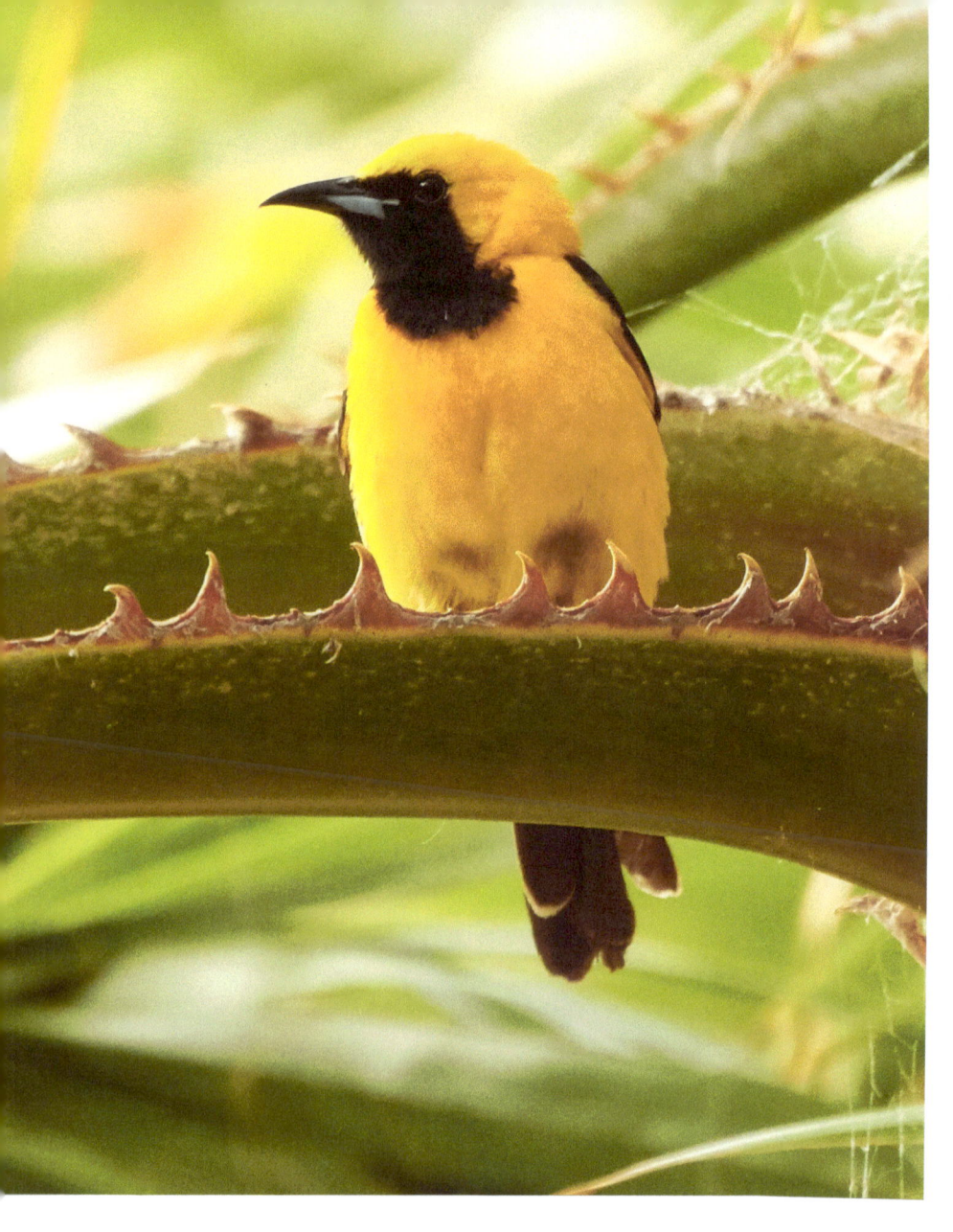

Hooded Oriole

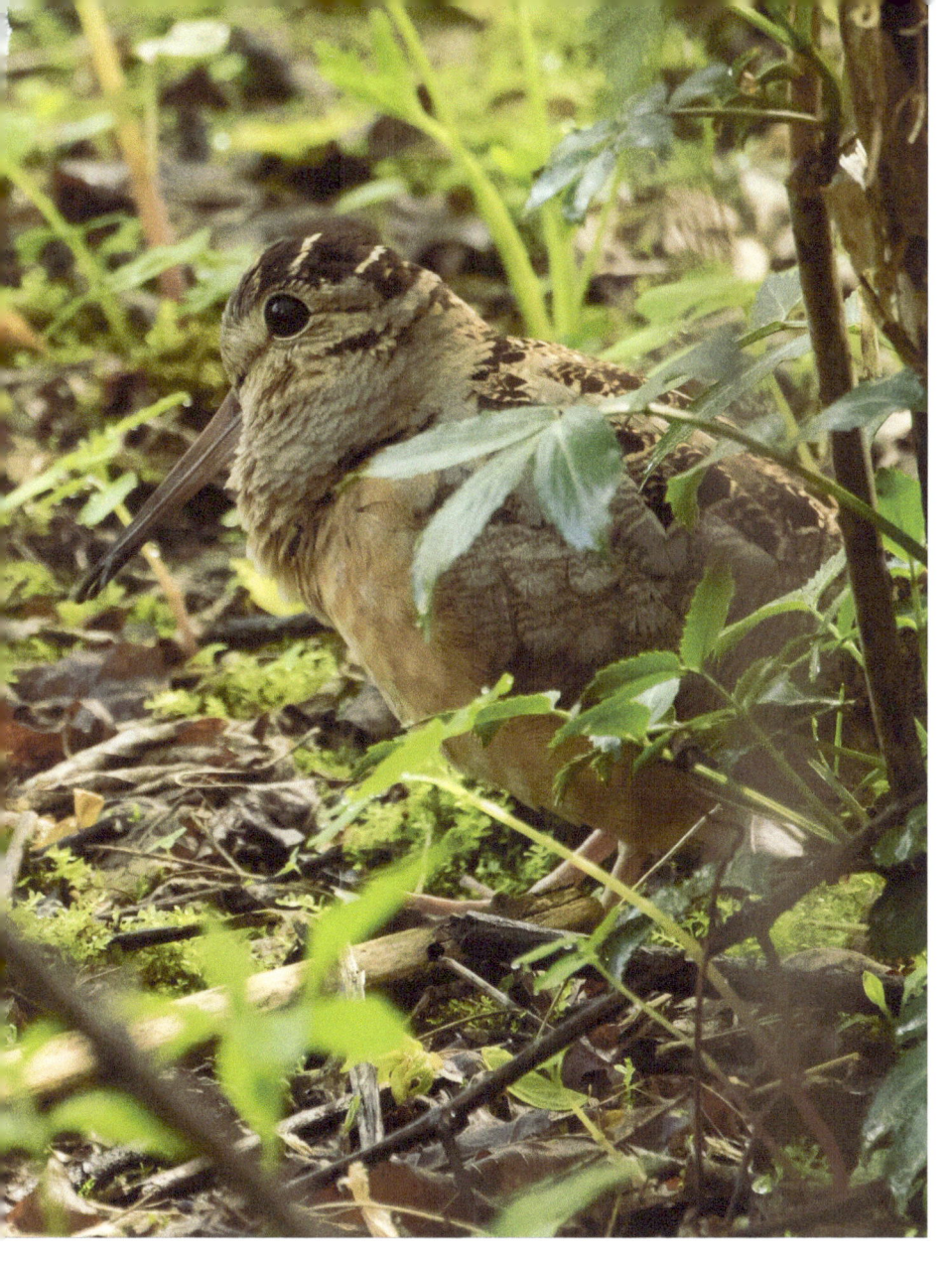

American Woodcock

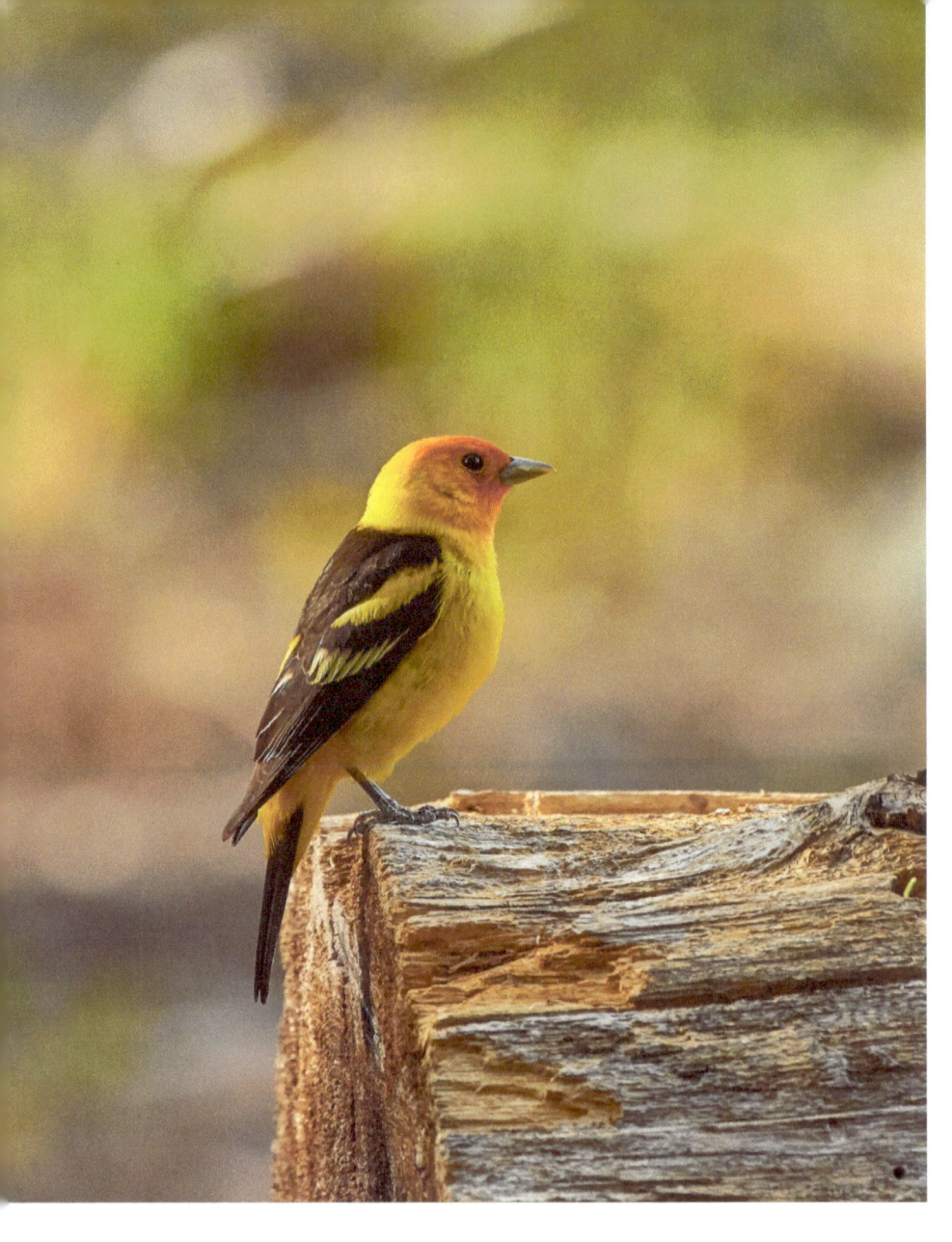

Western Tanager

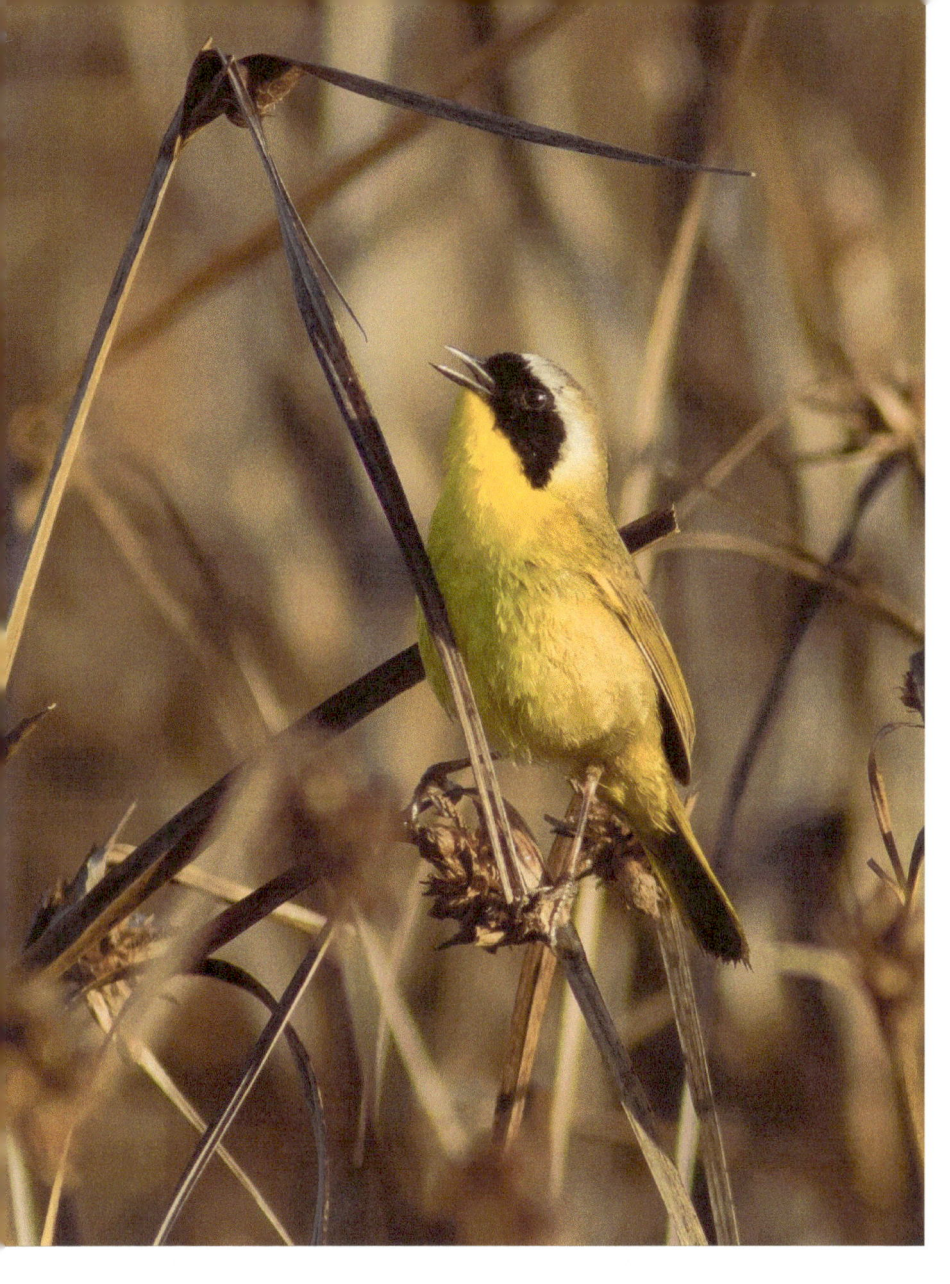

Common Yellowthroat

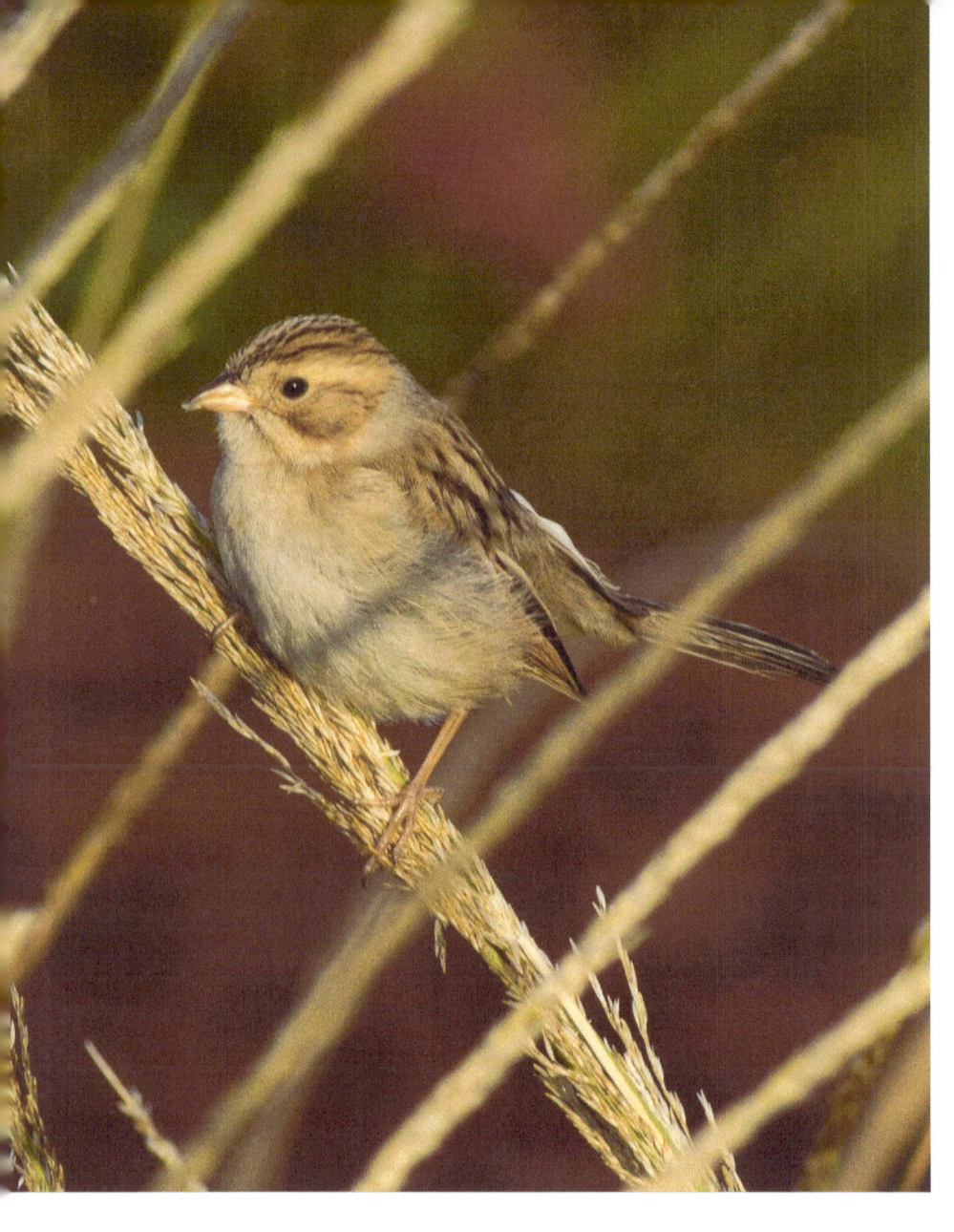

Clay-colored Sparrow

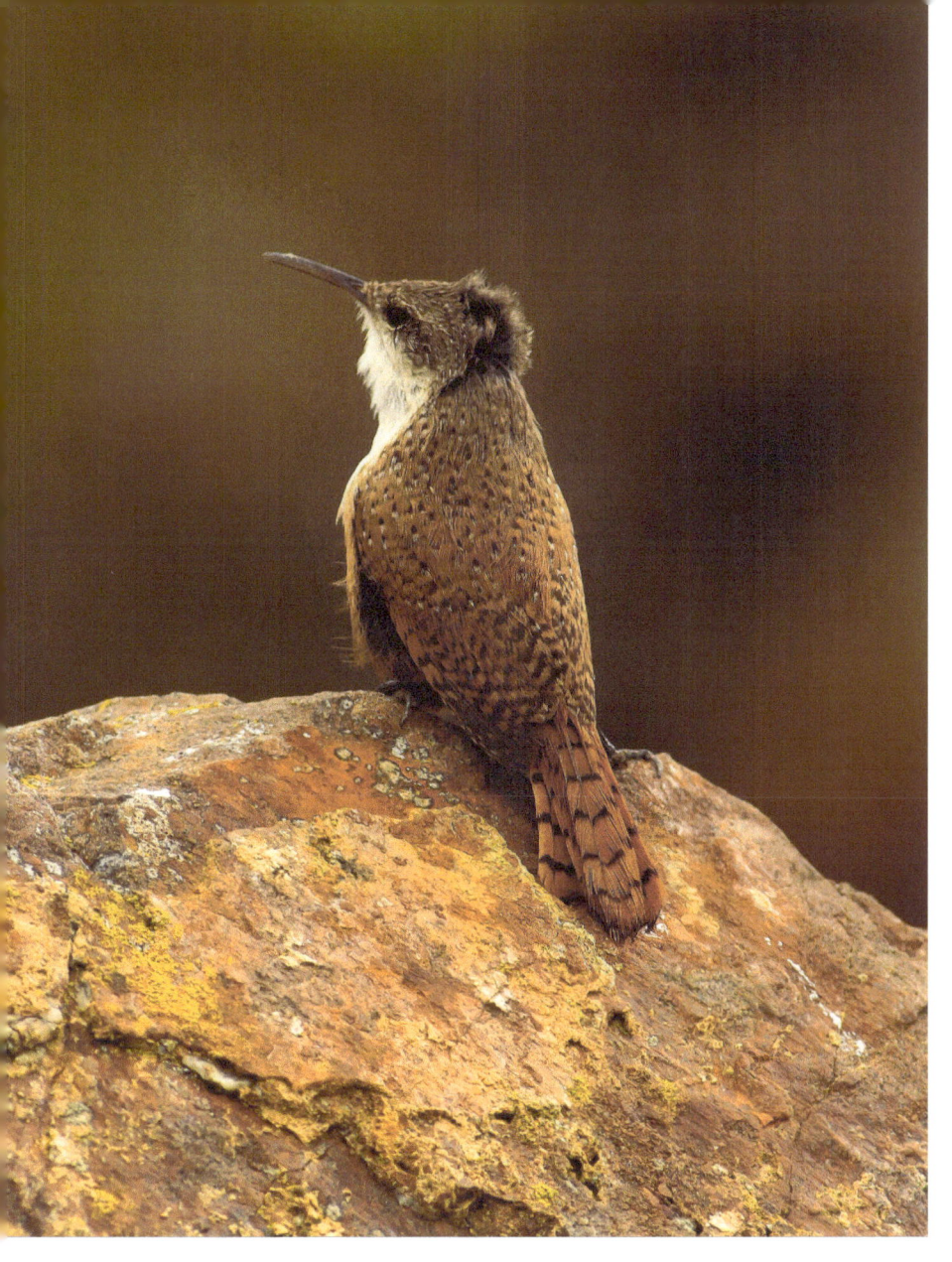

Canyon Wren

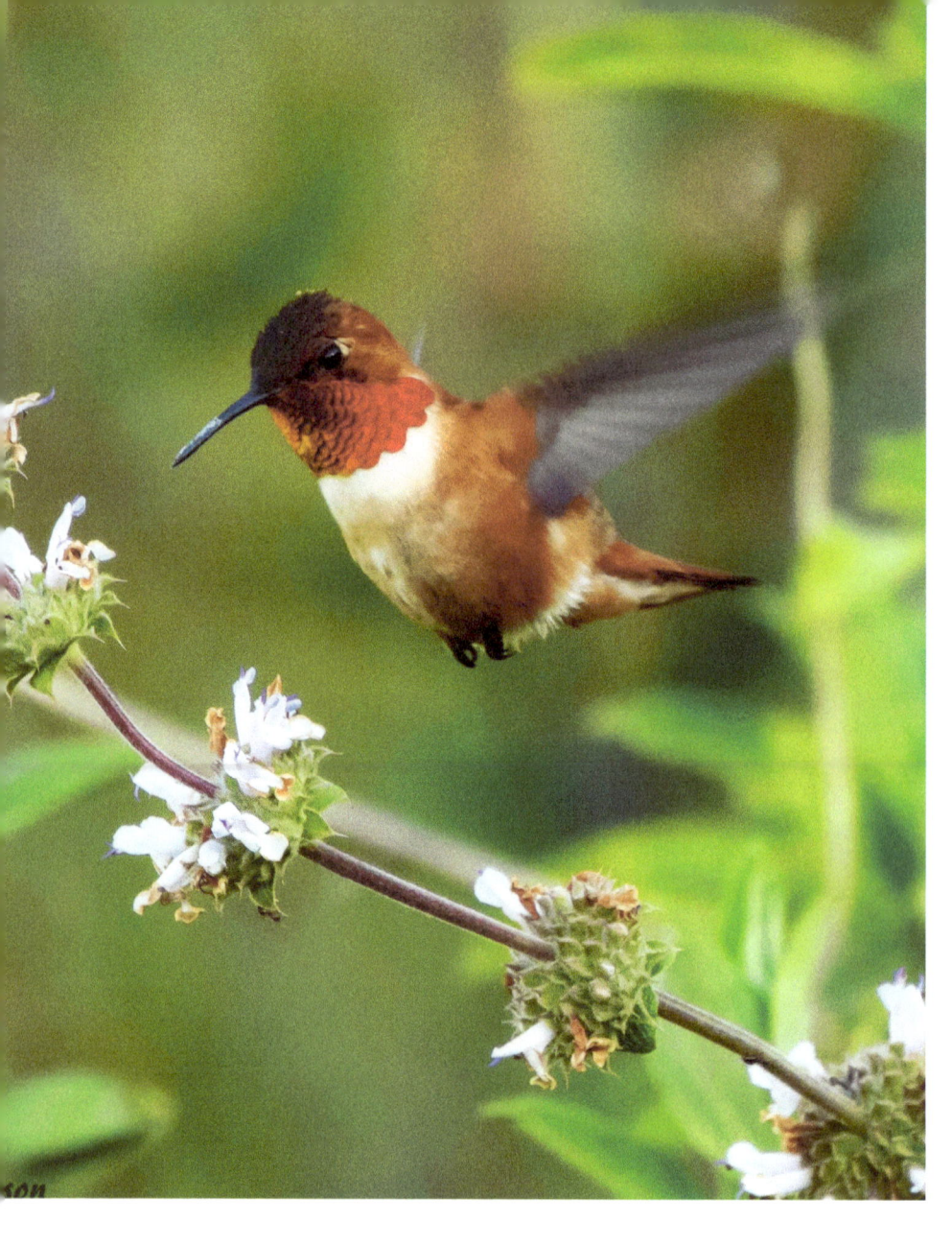

Rufous Hummingbird

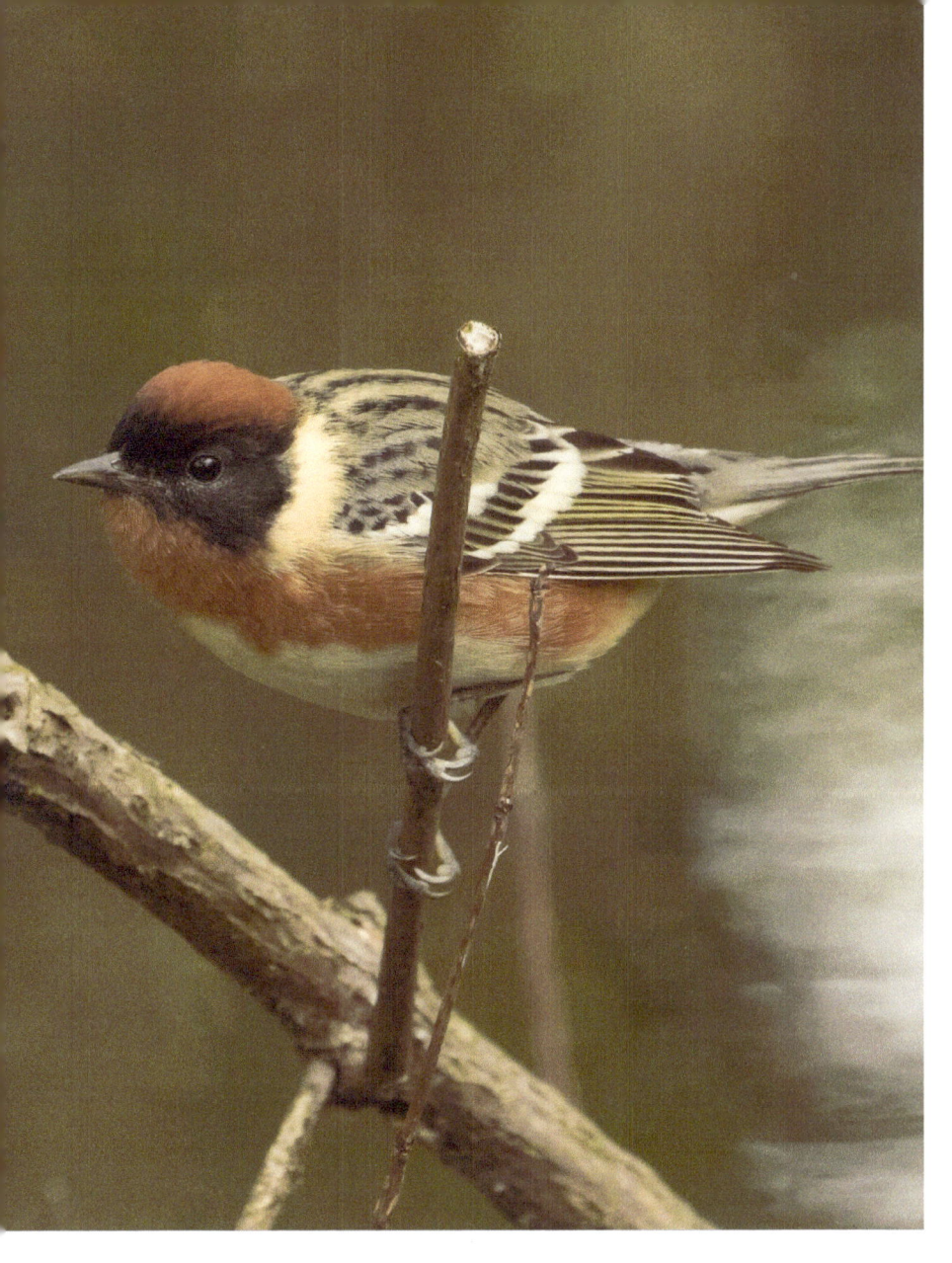

Bay-breasted Warbler

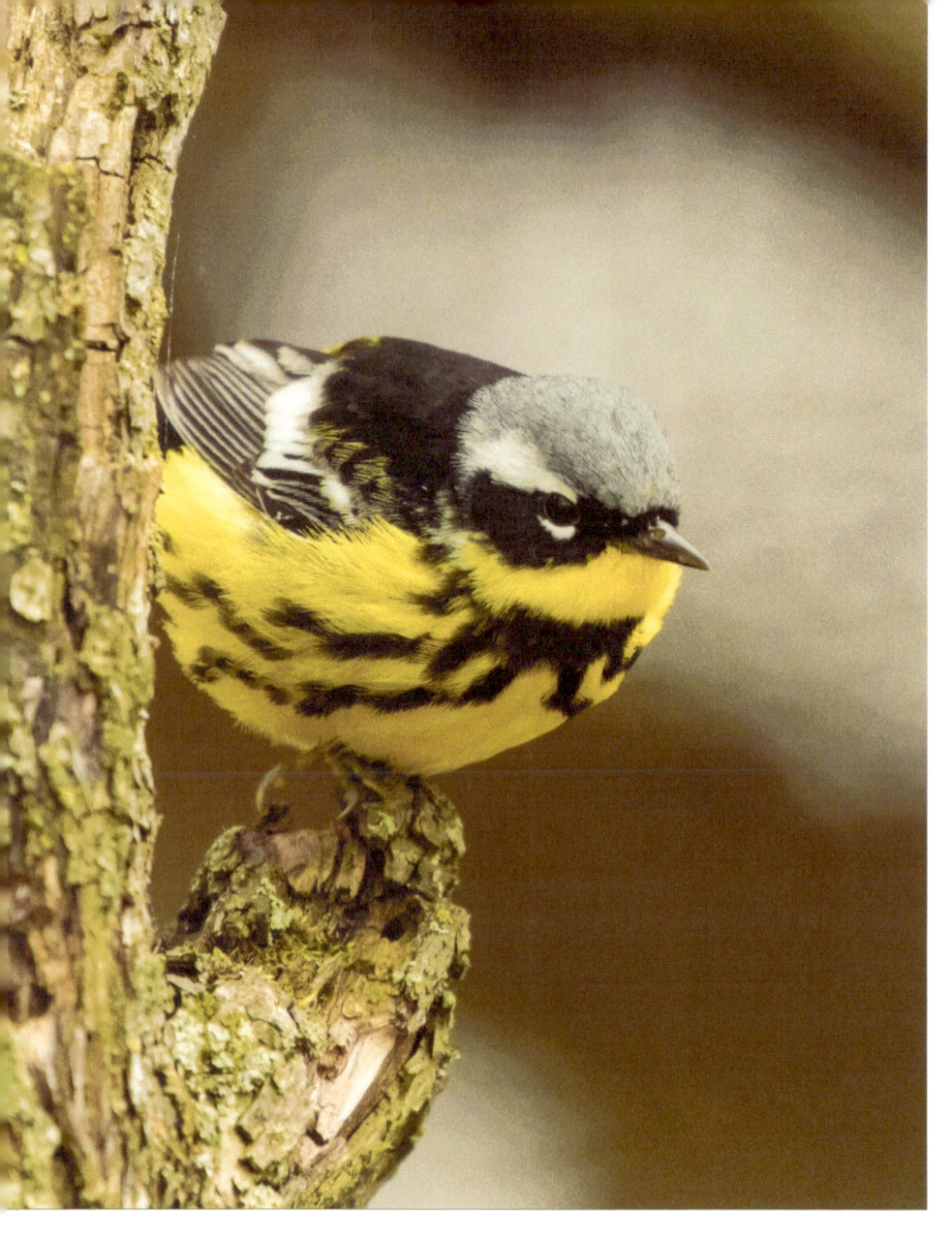

Magnolia Warbler

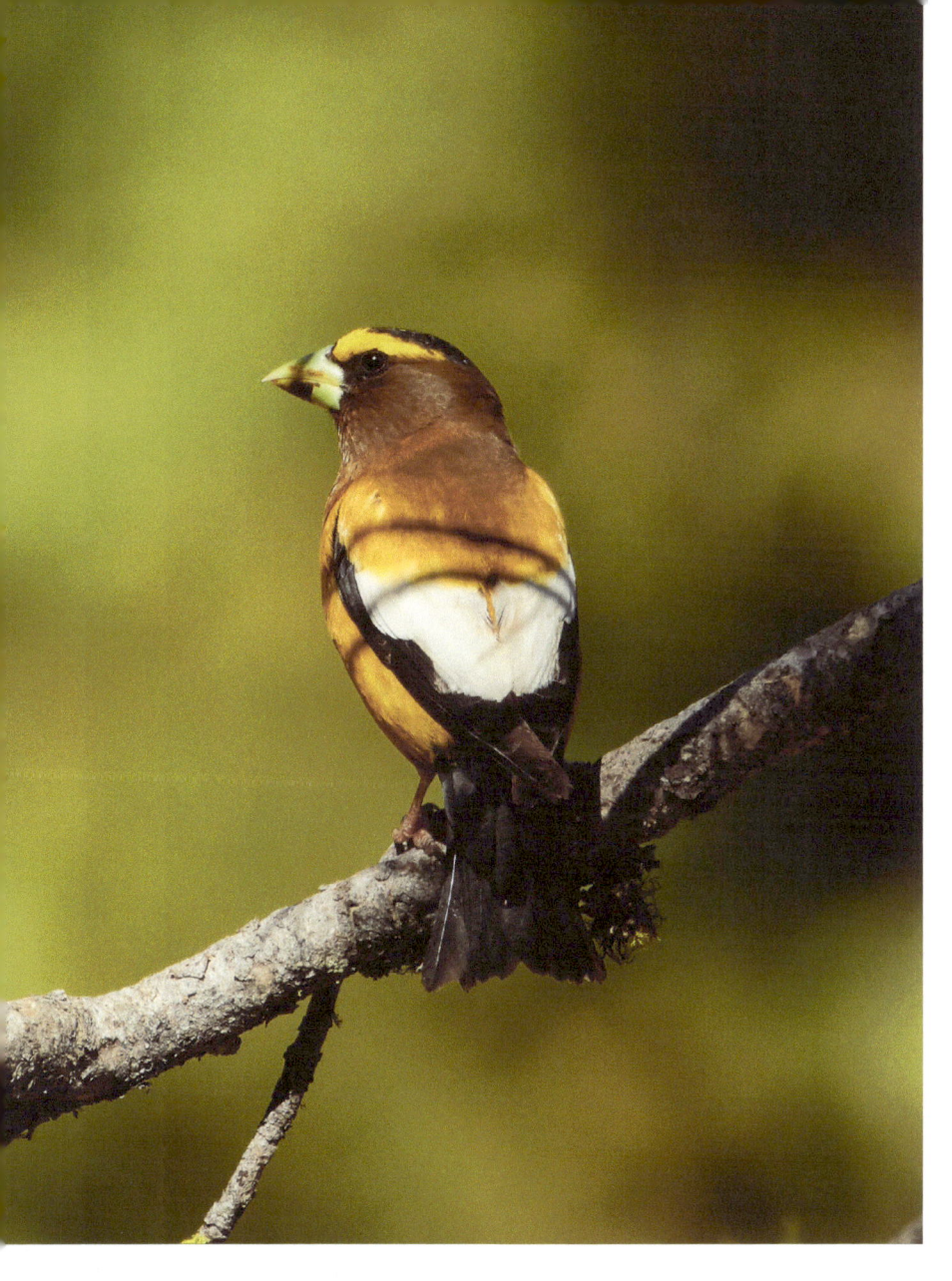

Evening Grosbeak

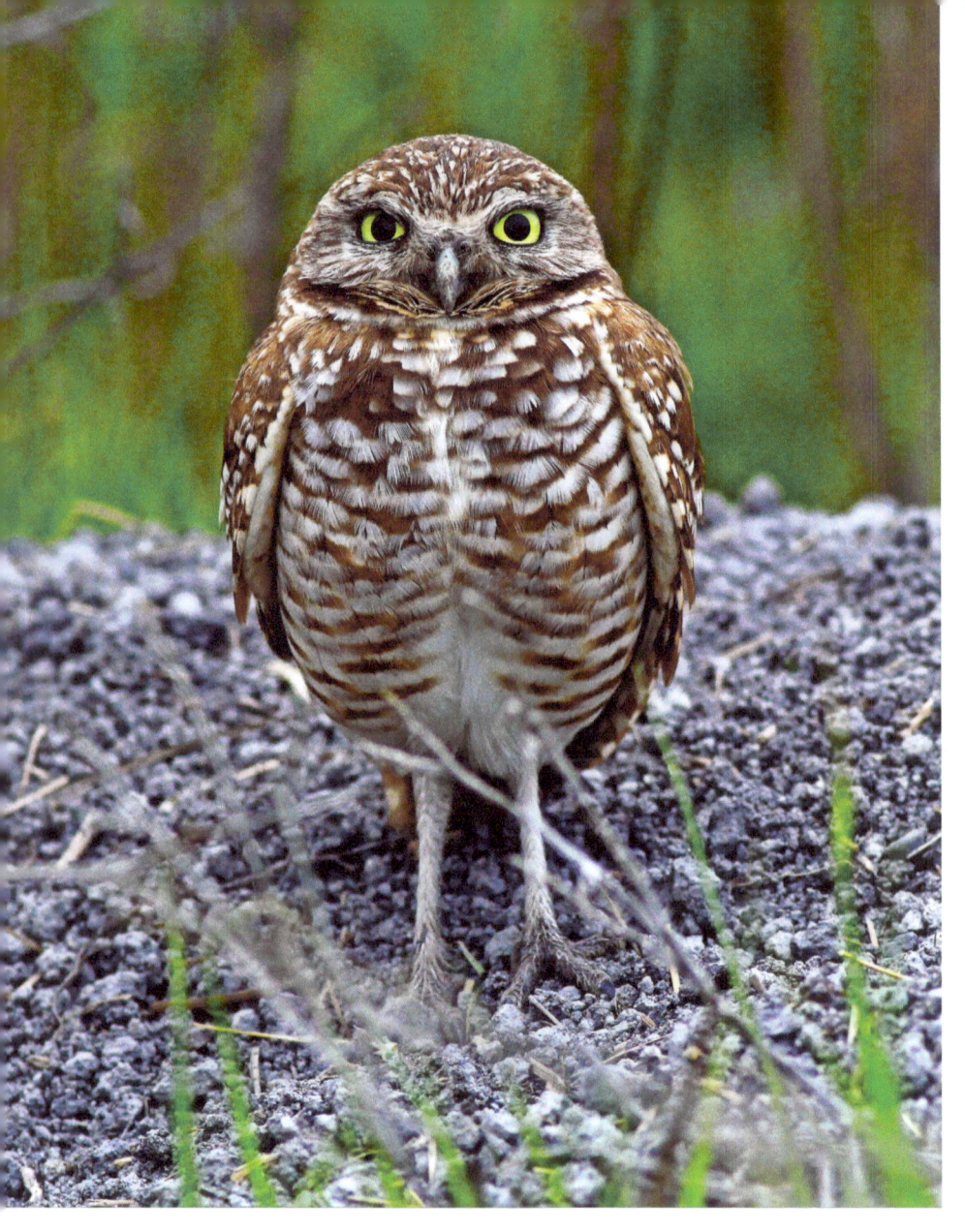

Burrowing Owl

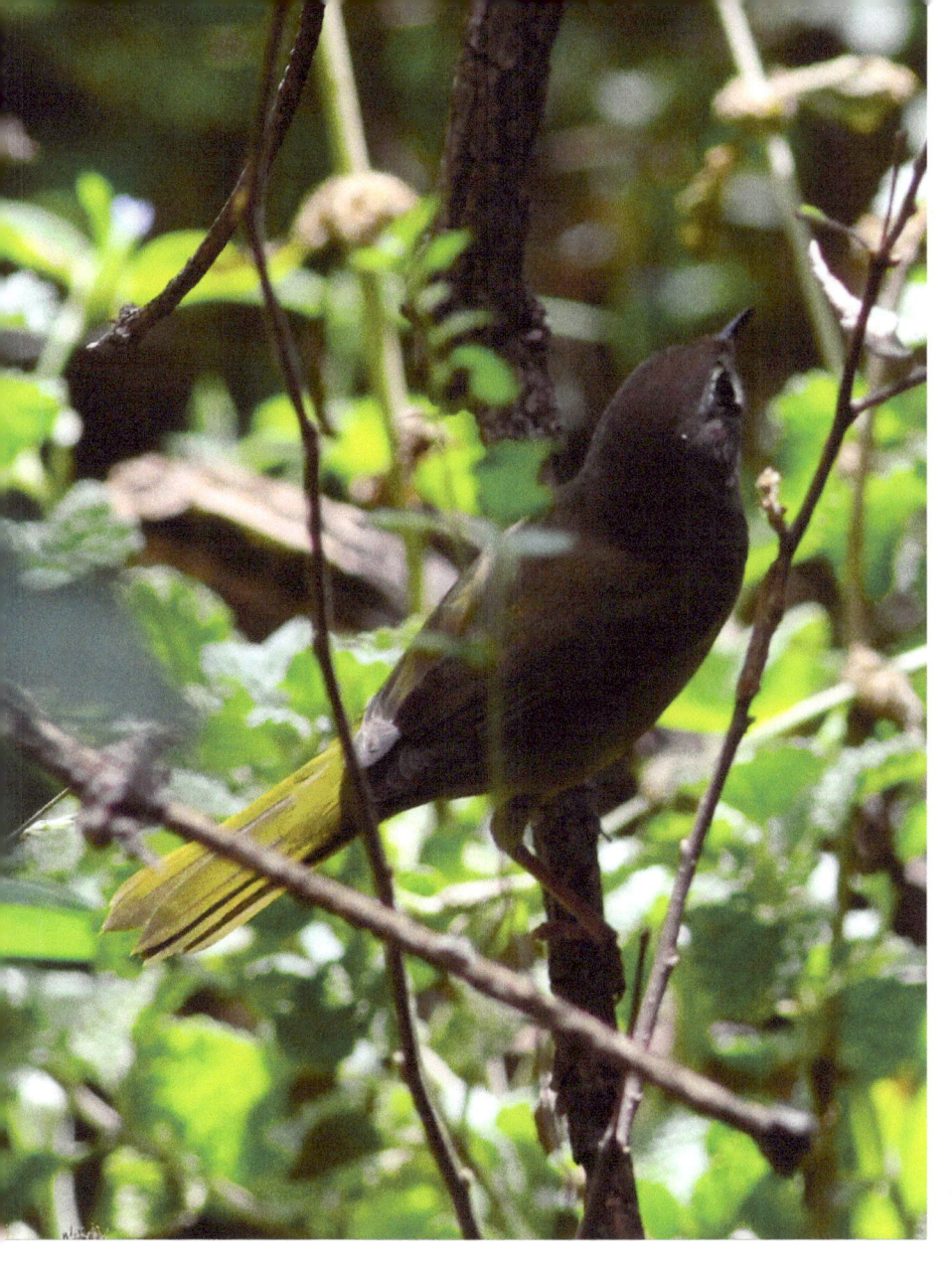

MacGillivray's Warbler

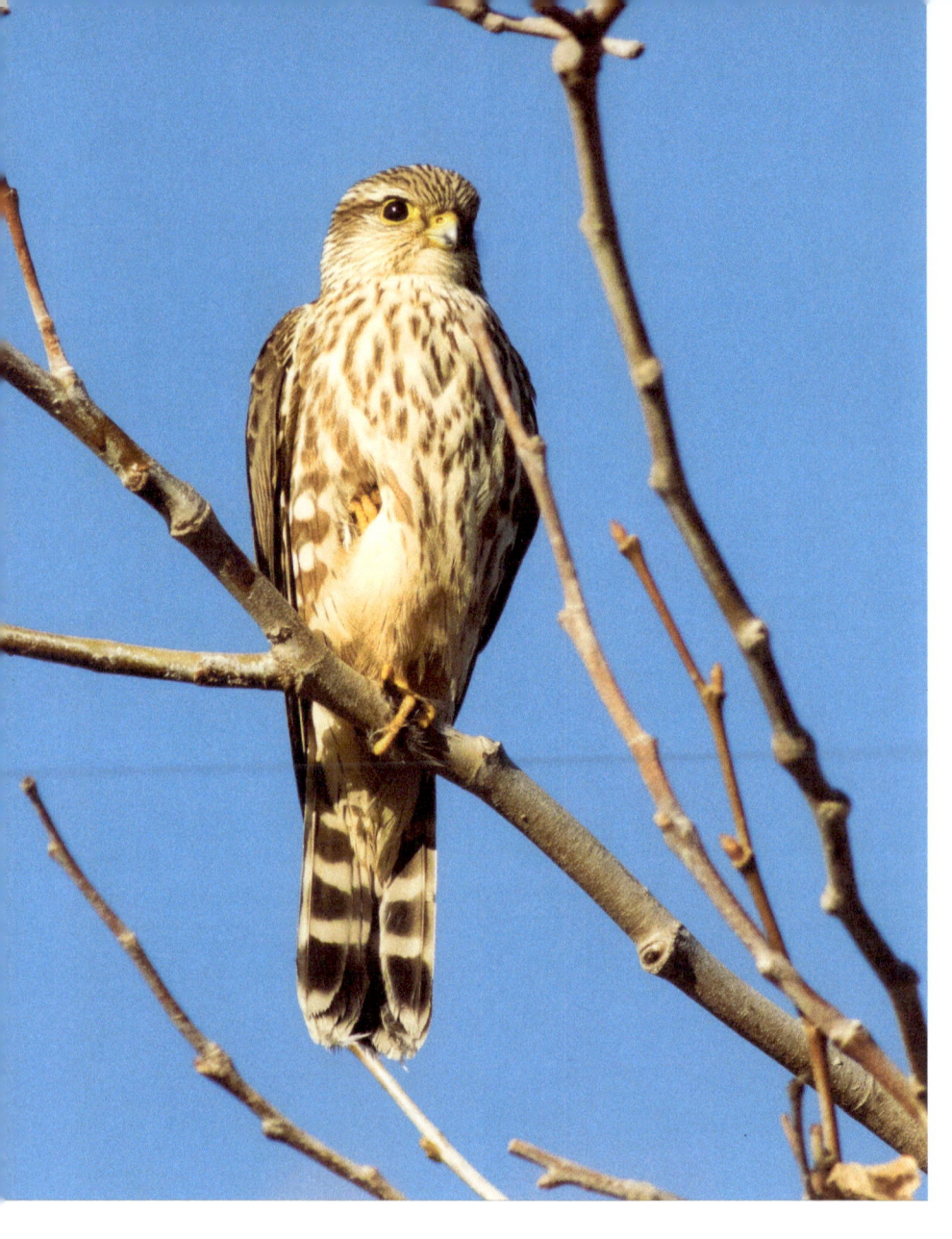

Merlin

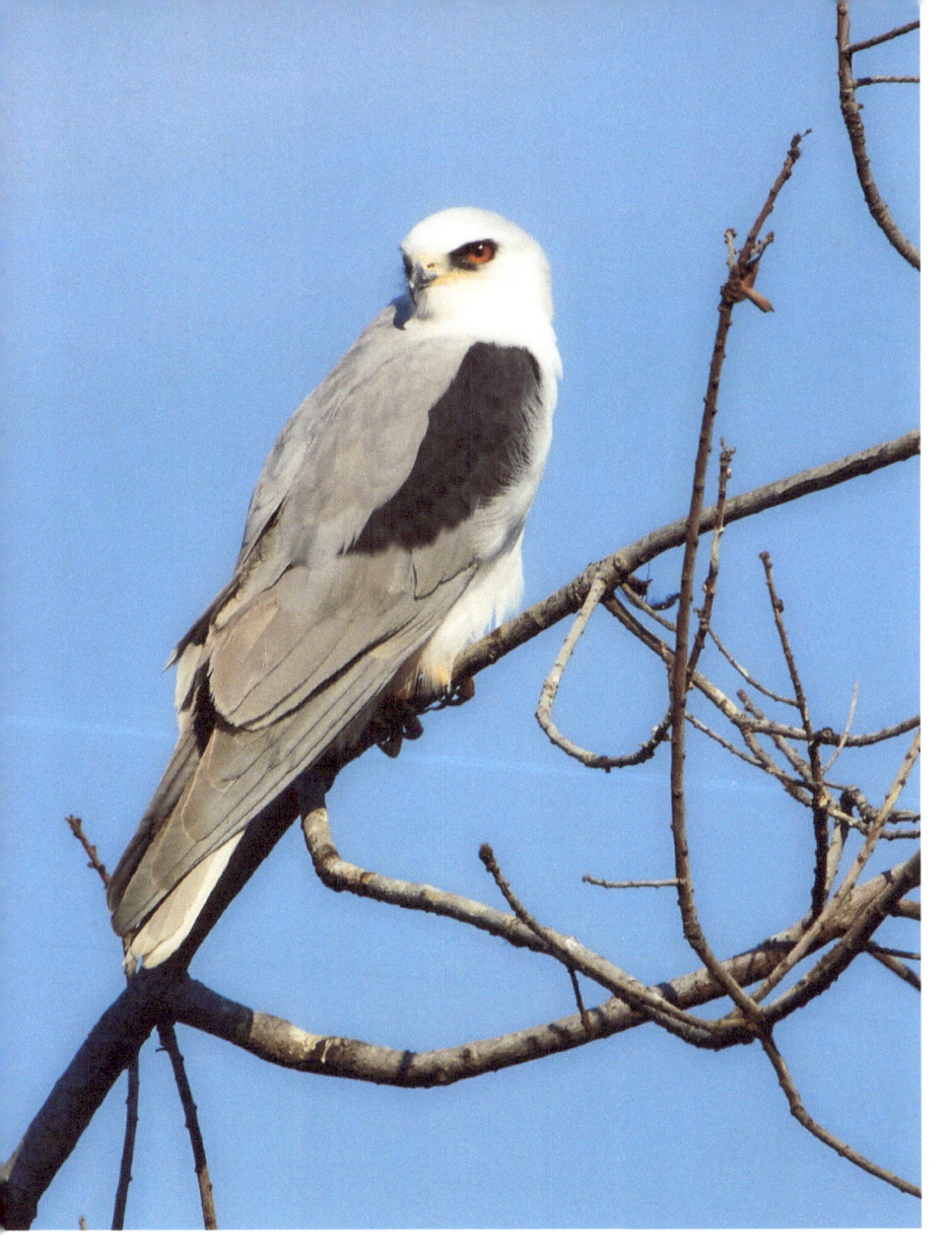

White-tailed Kite

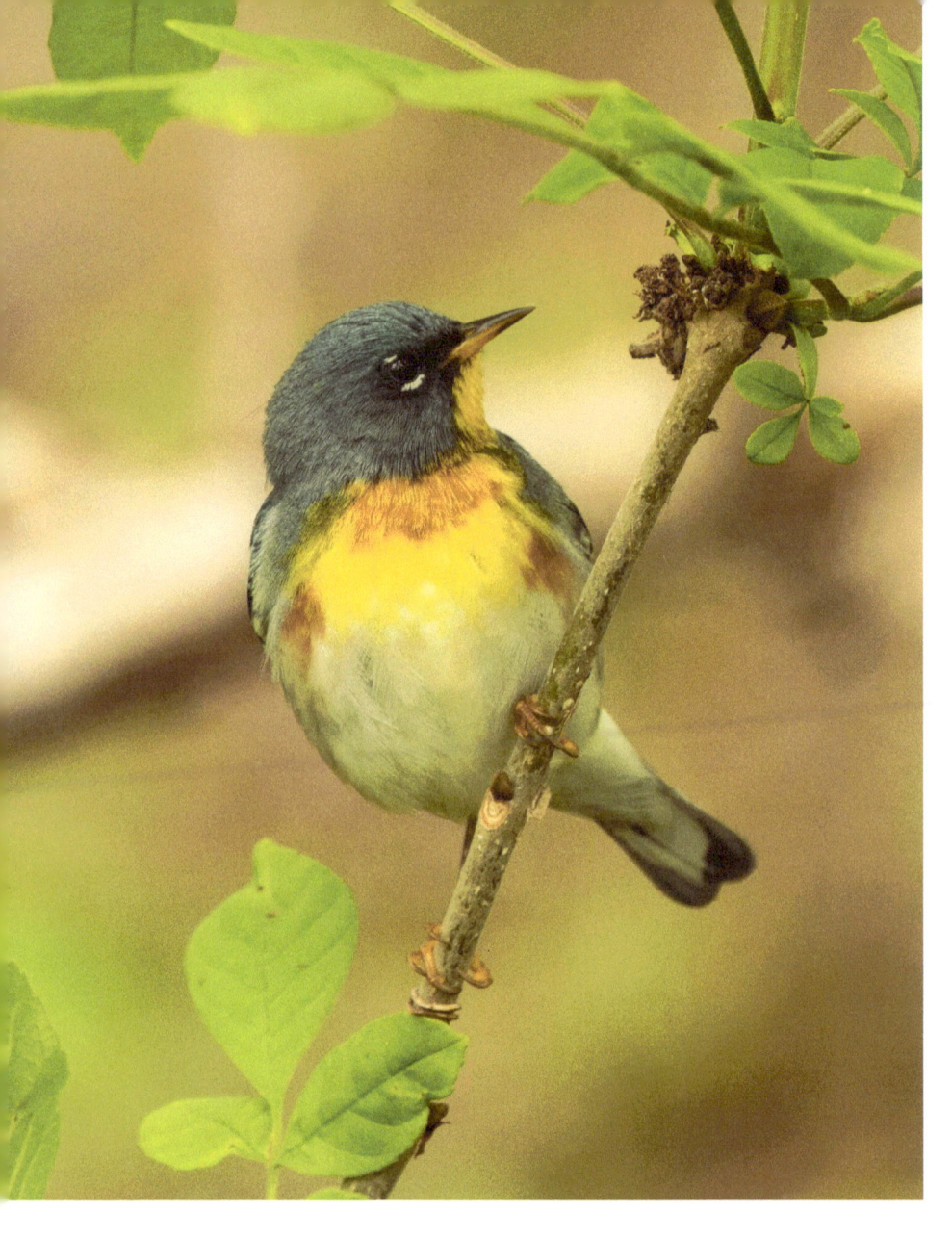

Northern Parula

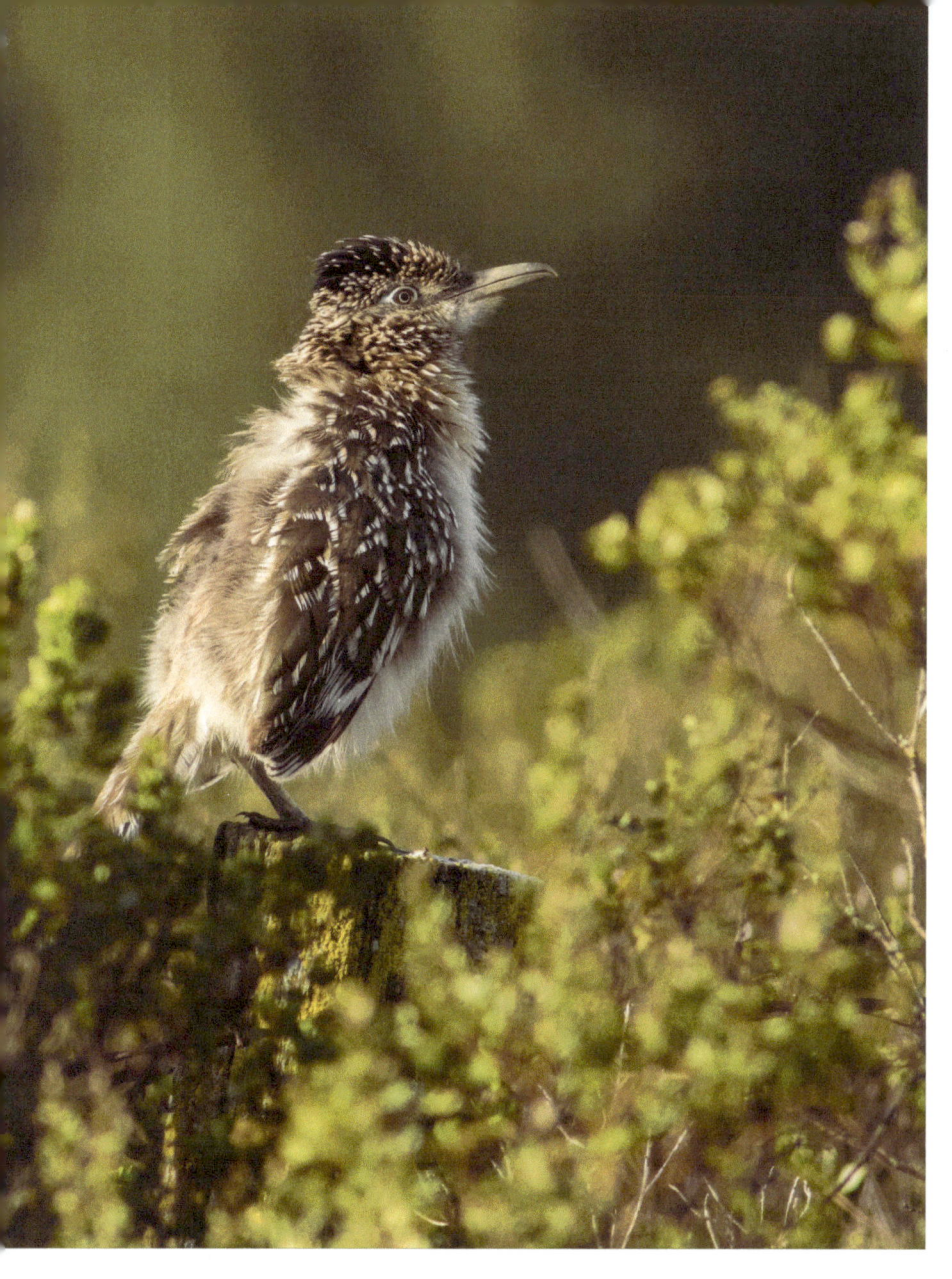

Greater Roadrunner

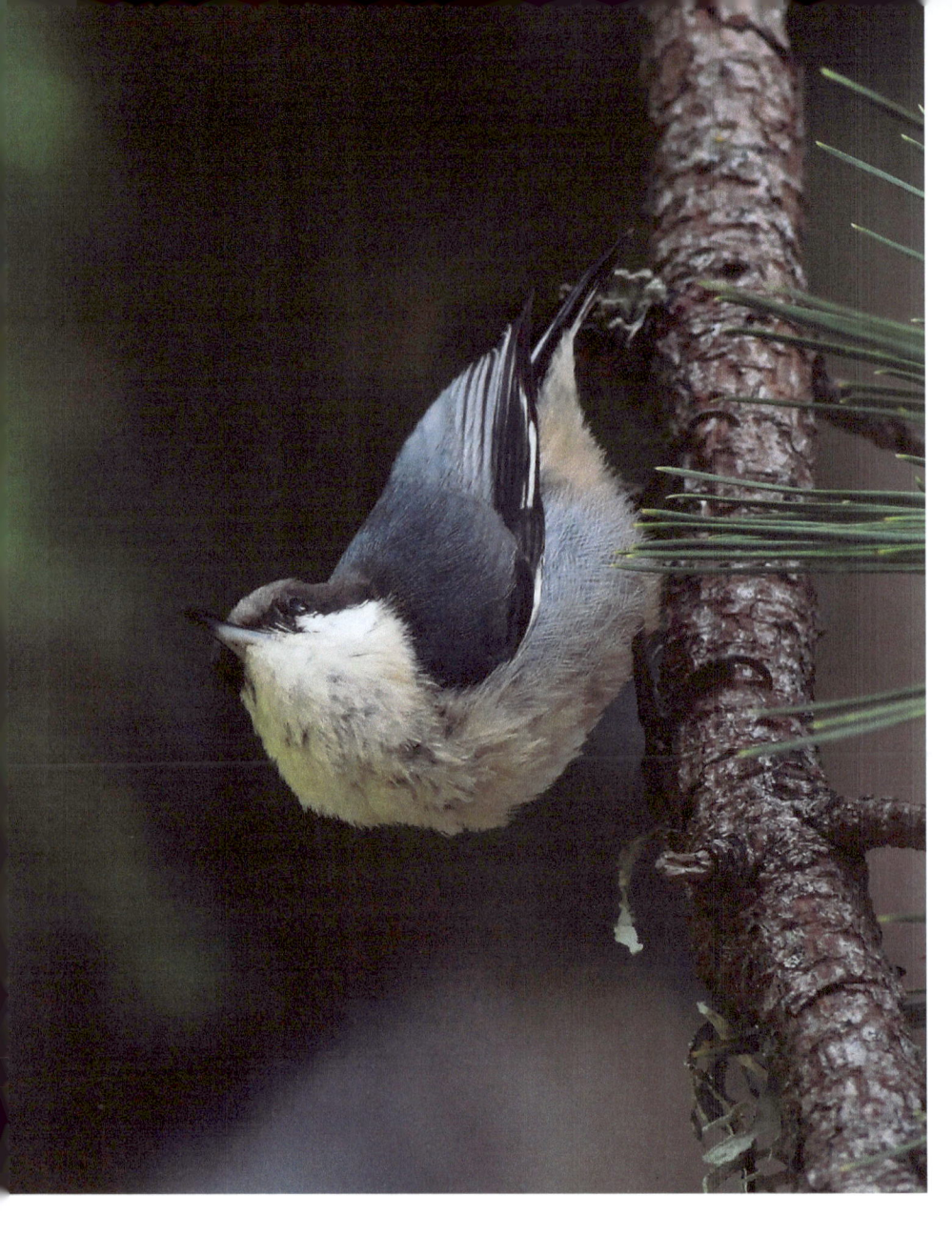

Pygmy Nuthatch

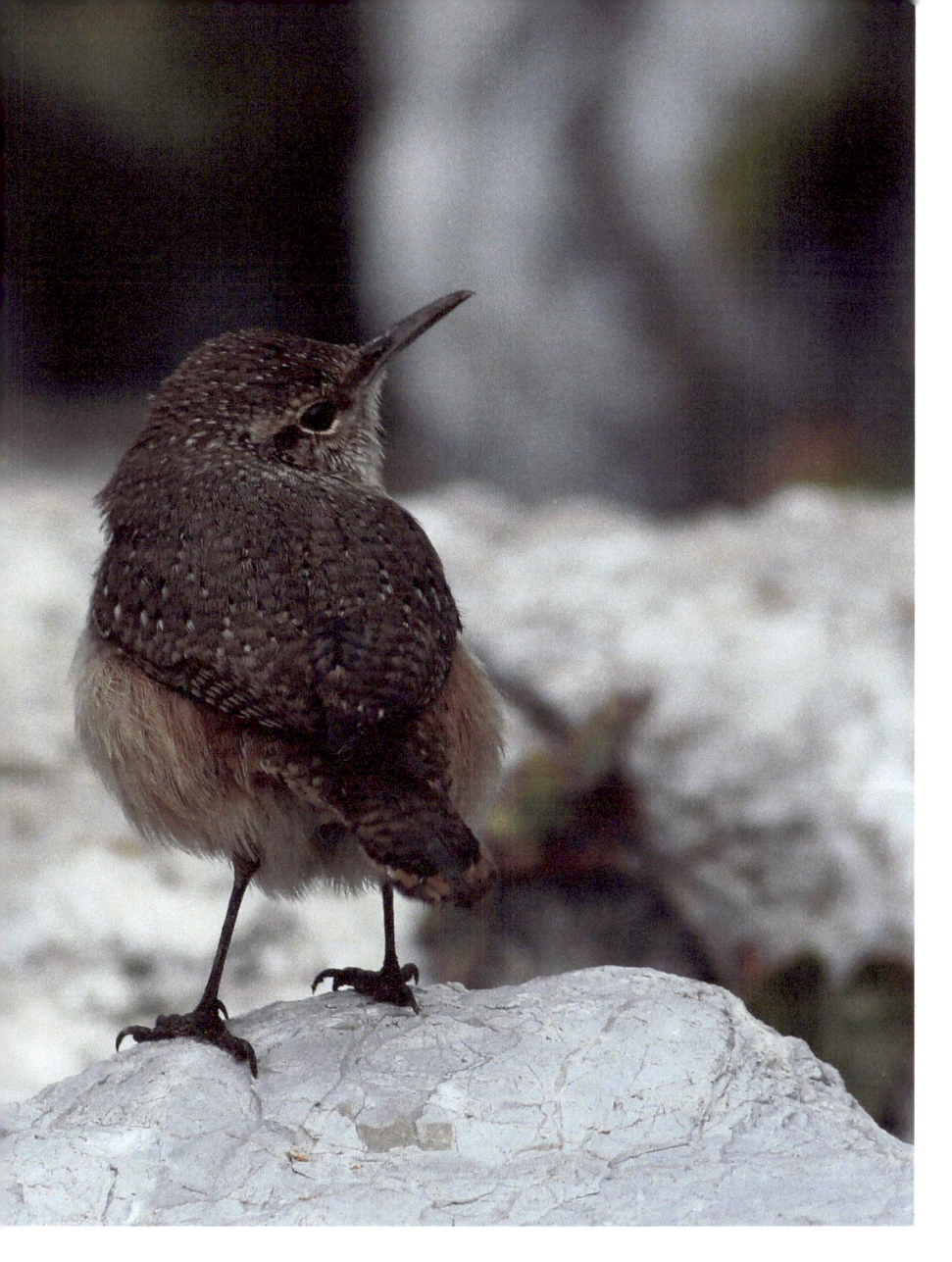

Rock Wren

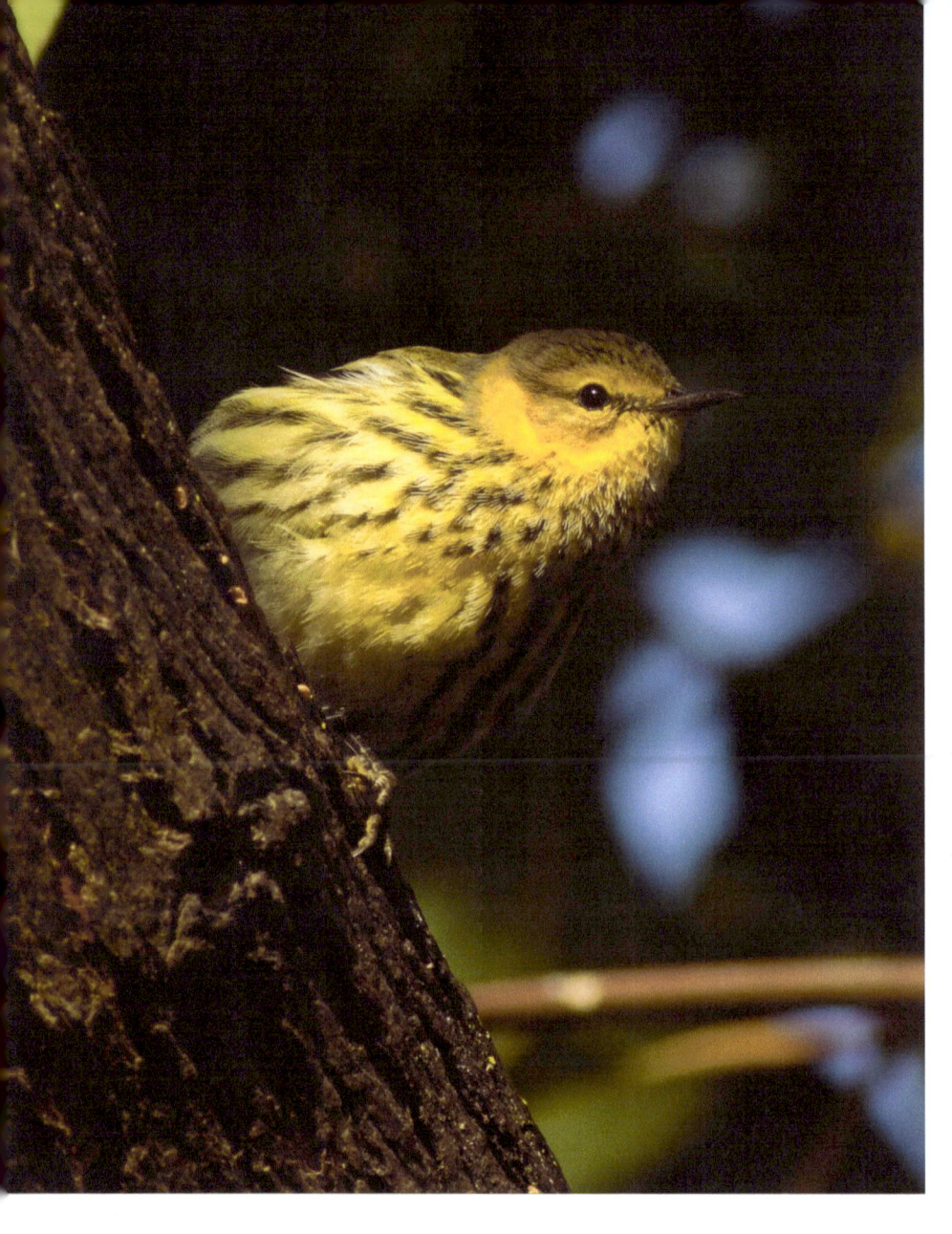

Cape May Warbler

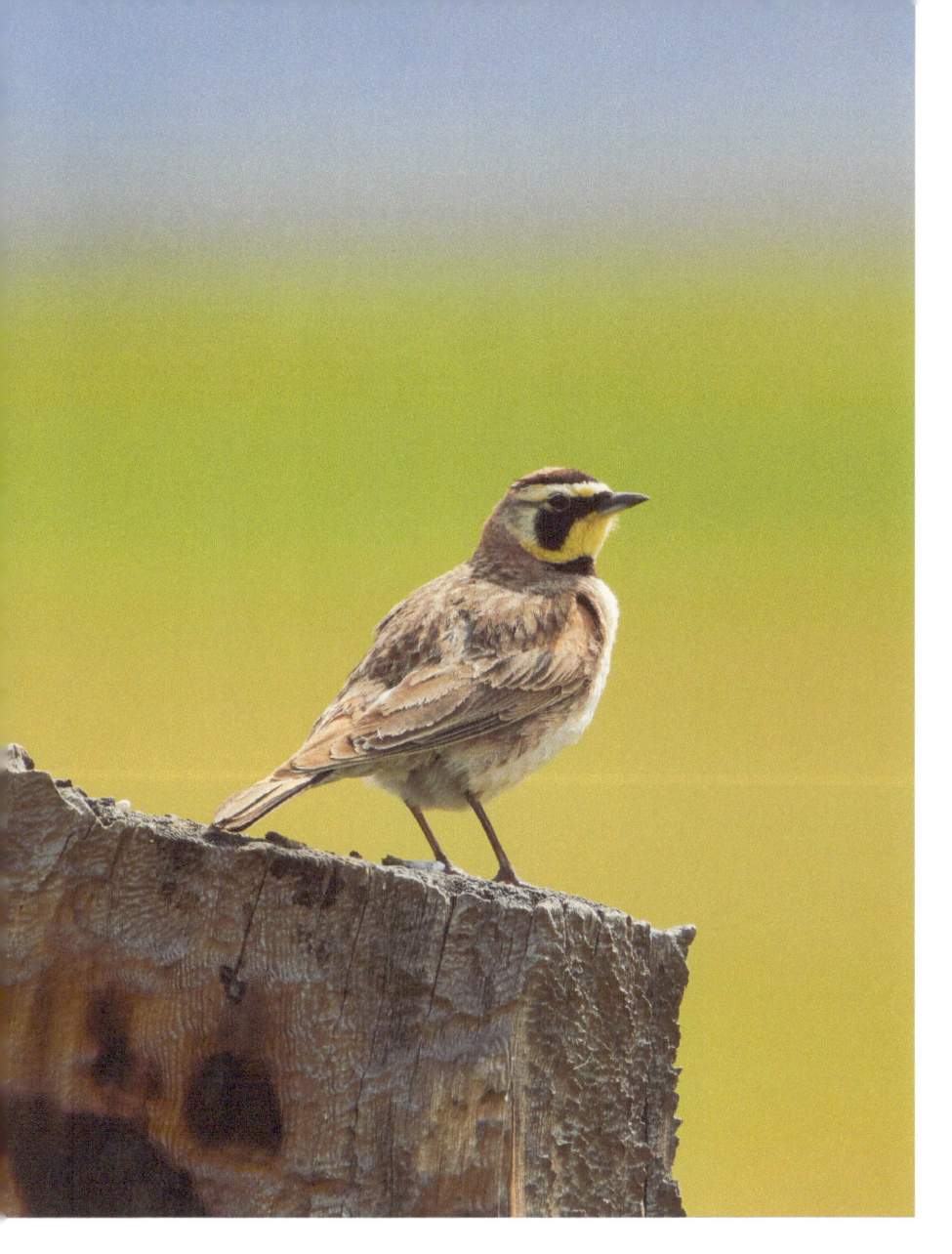

Horned Lark

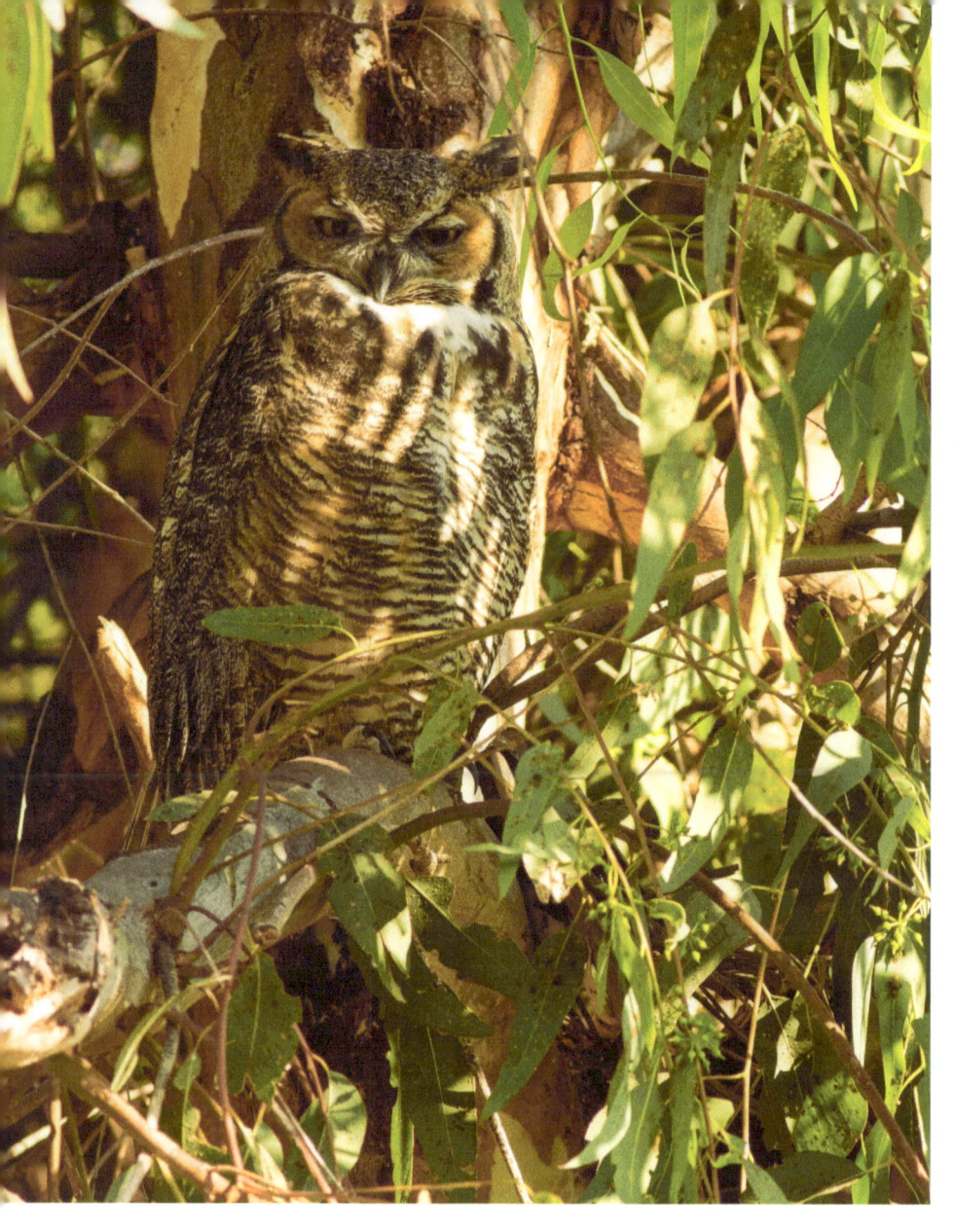

Great Horned Owl

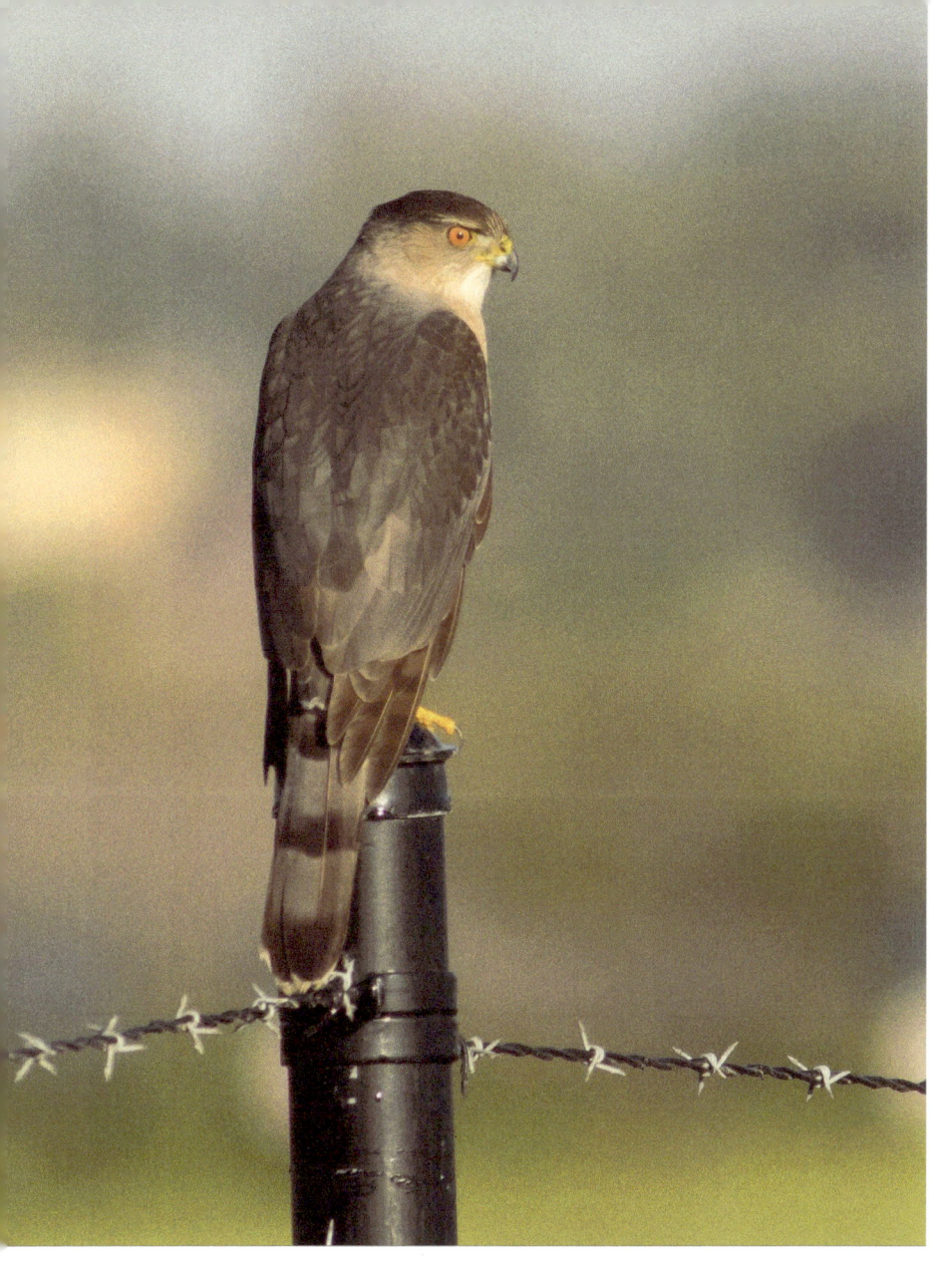

Cooper's Hawk

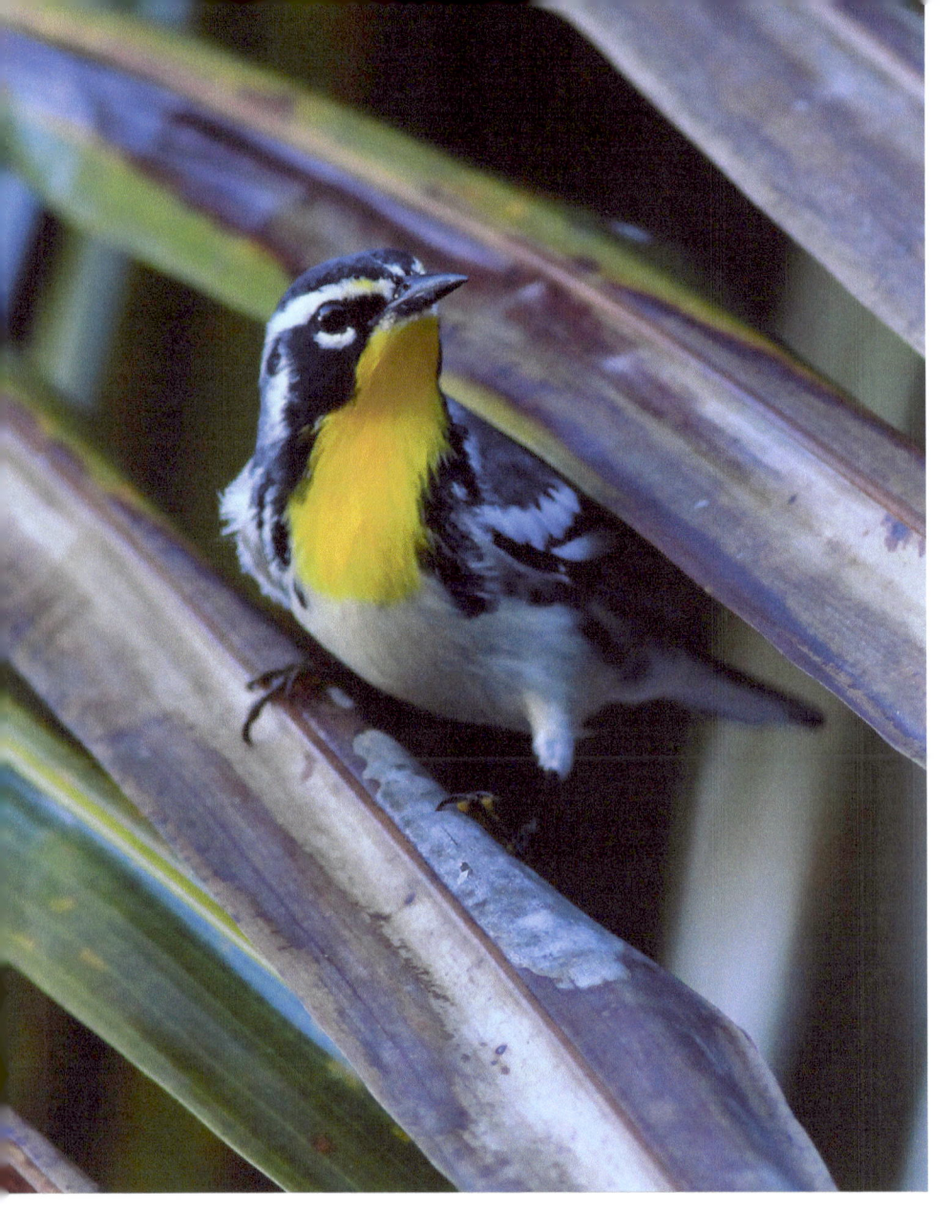

Yellow-throated Warbler

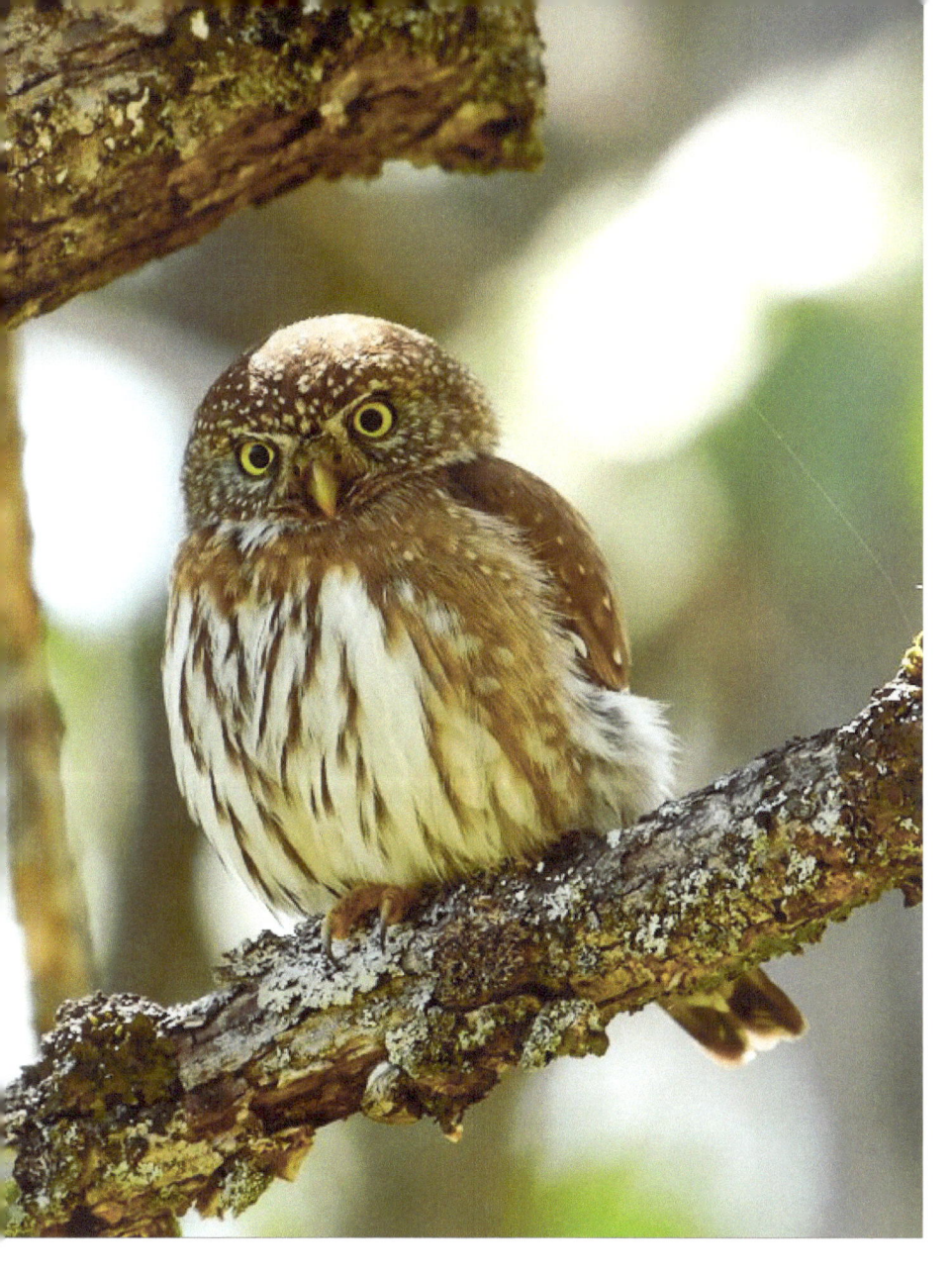

Northern Pygmy Owl

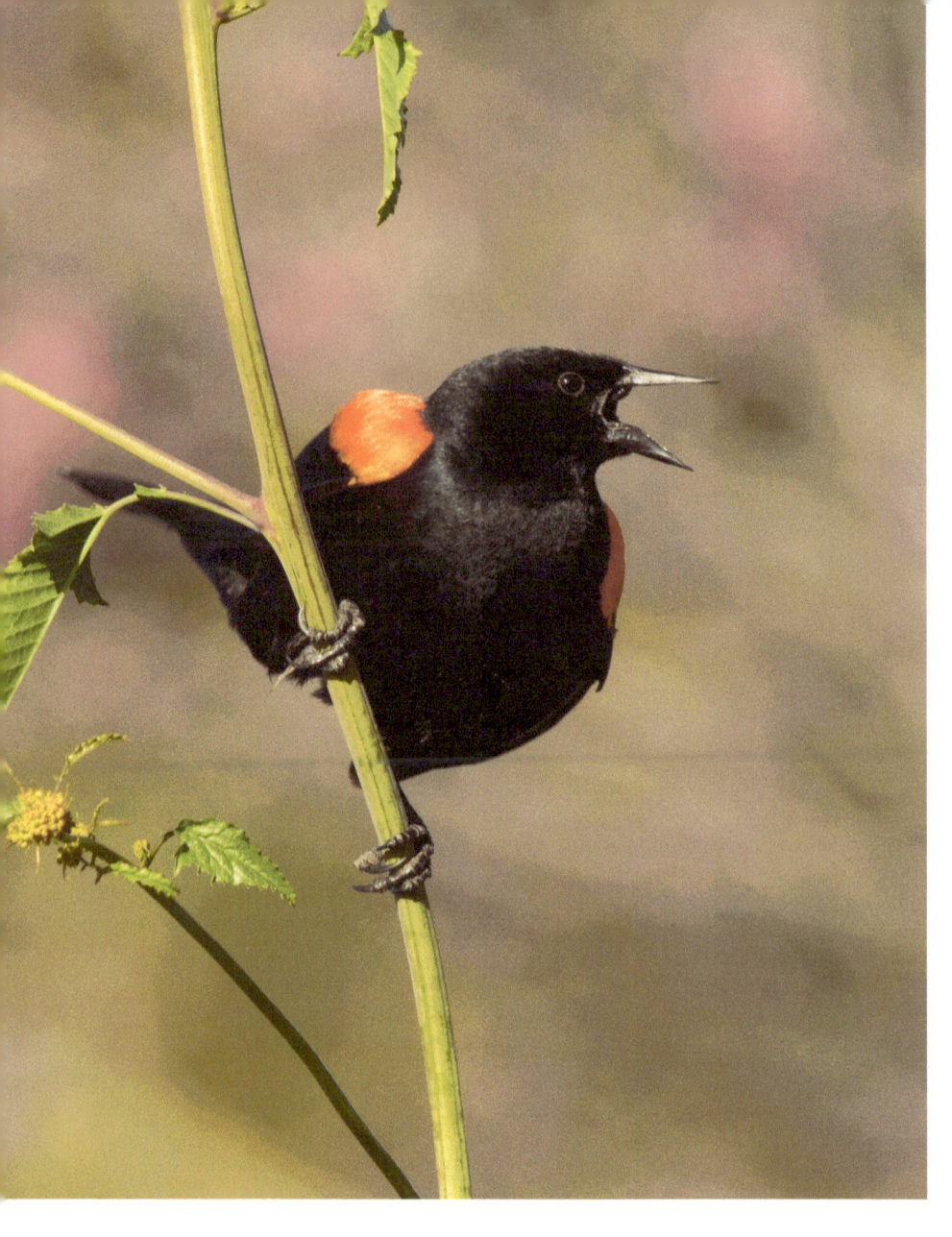

Red-winged Blackbird

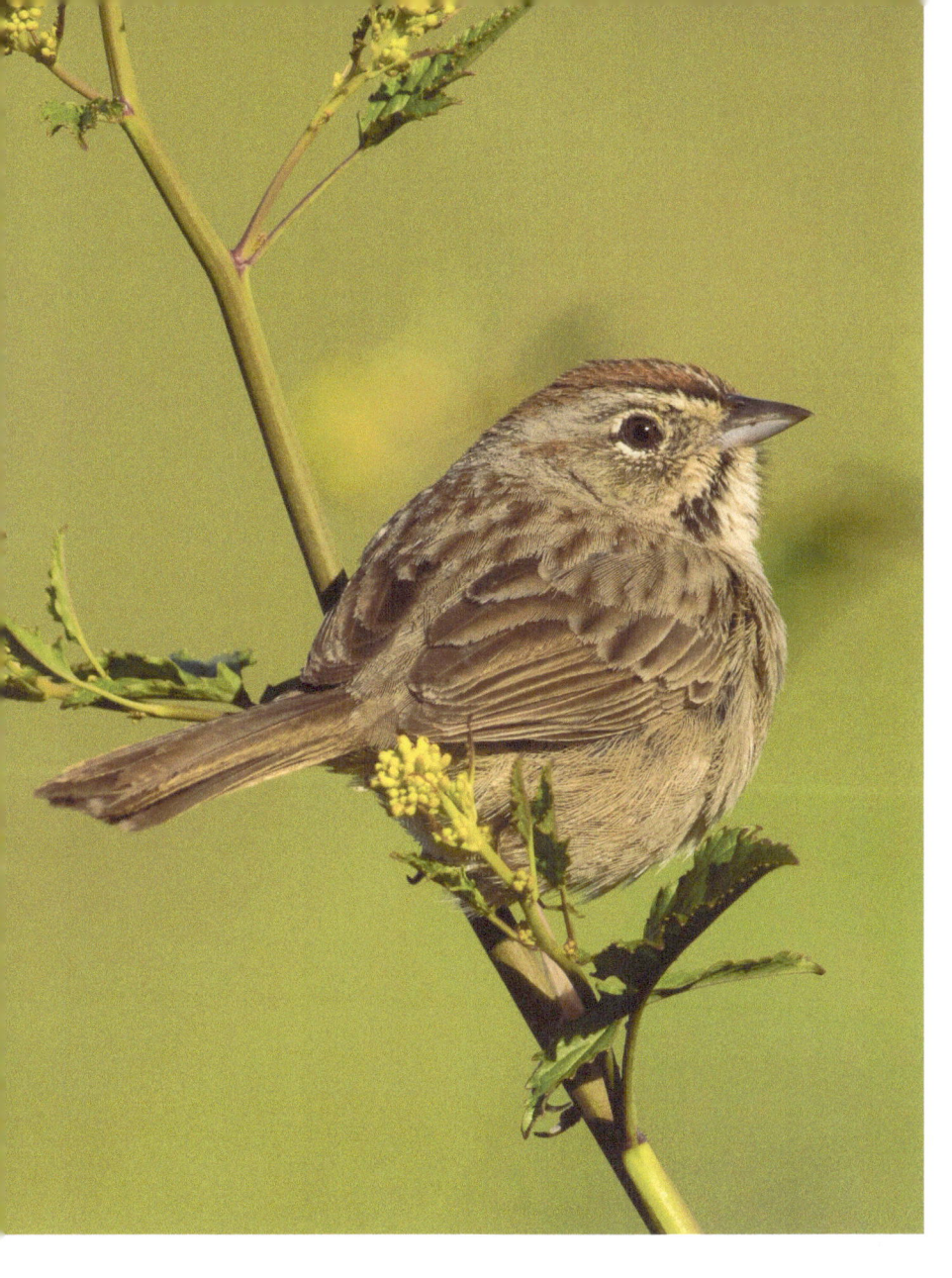

Rufous-crowned Sparrow

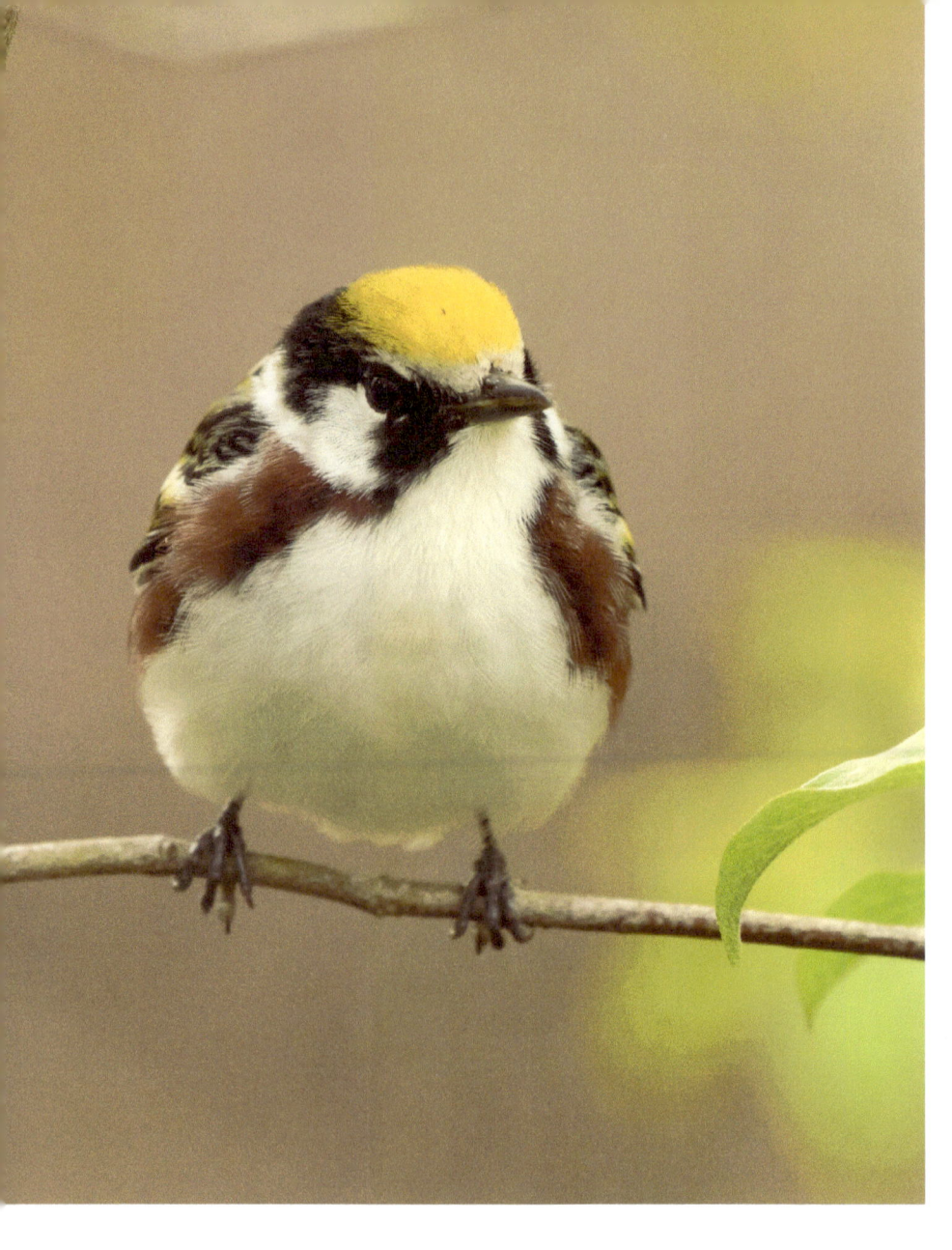

Chestnut-sided Warbler

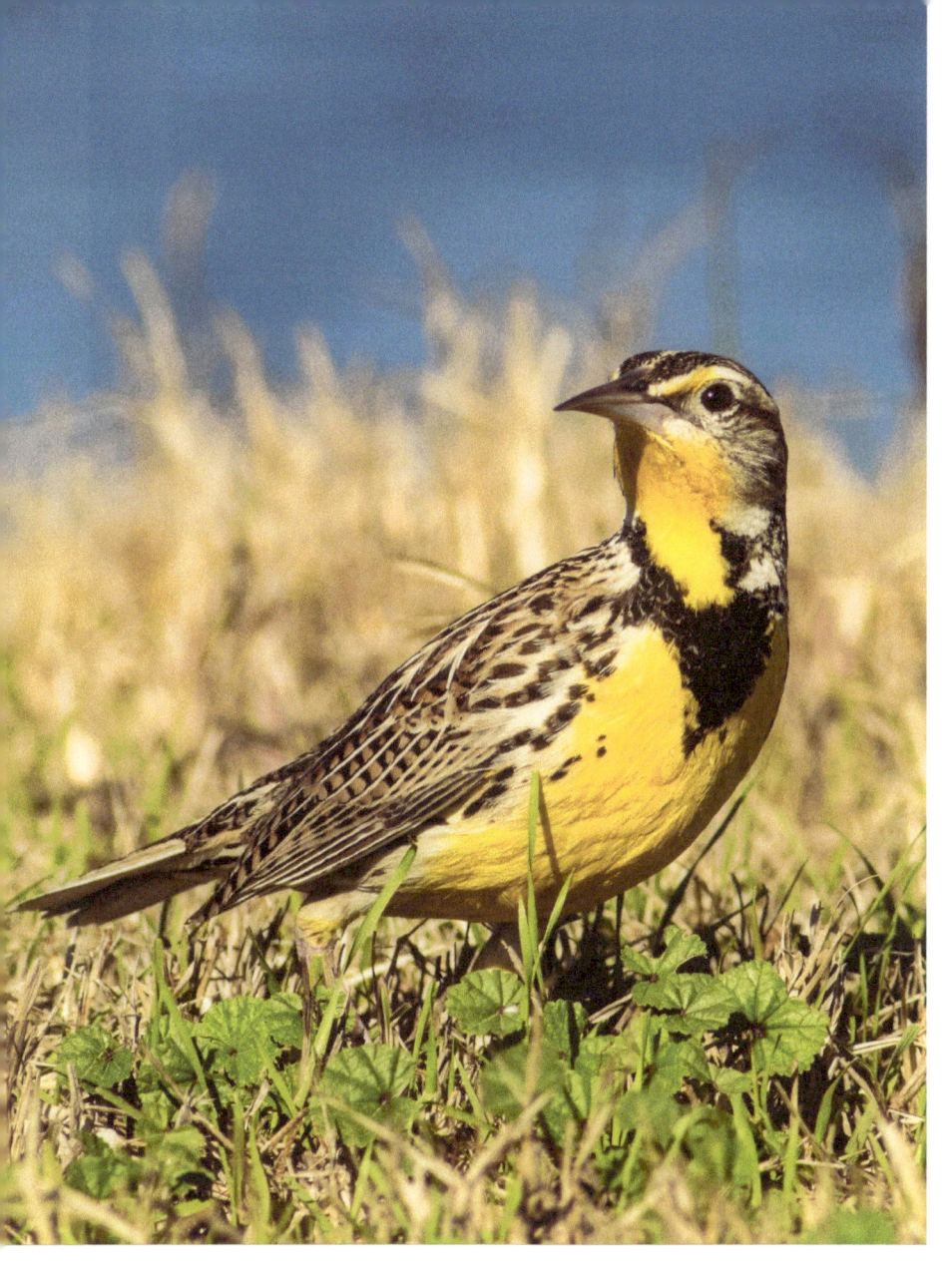

Western Meadowlark

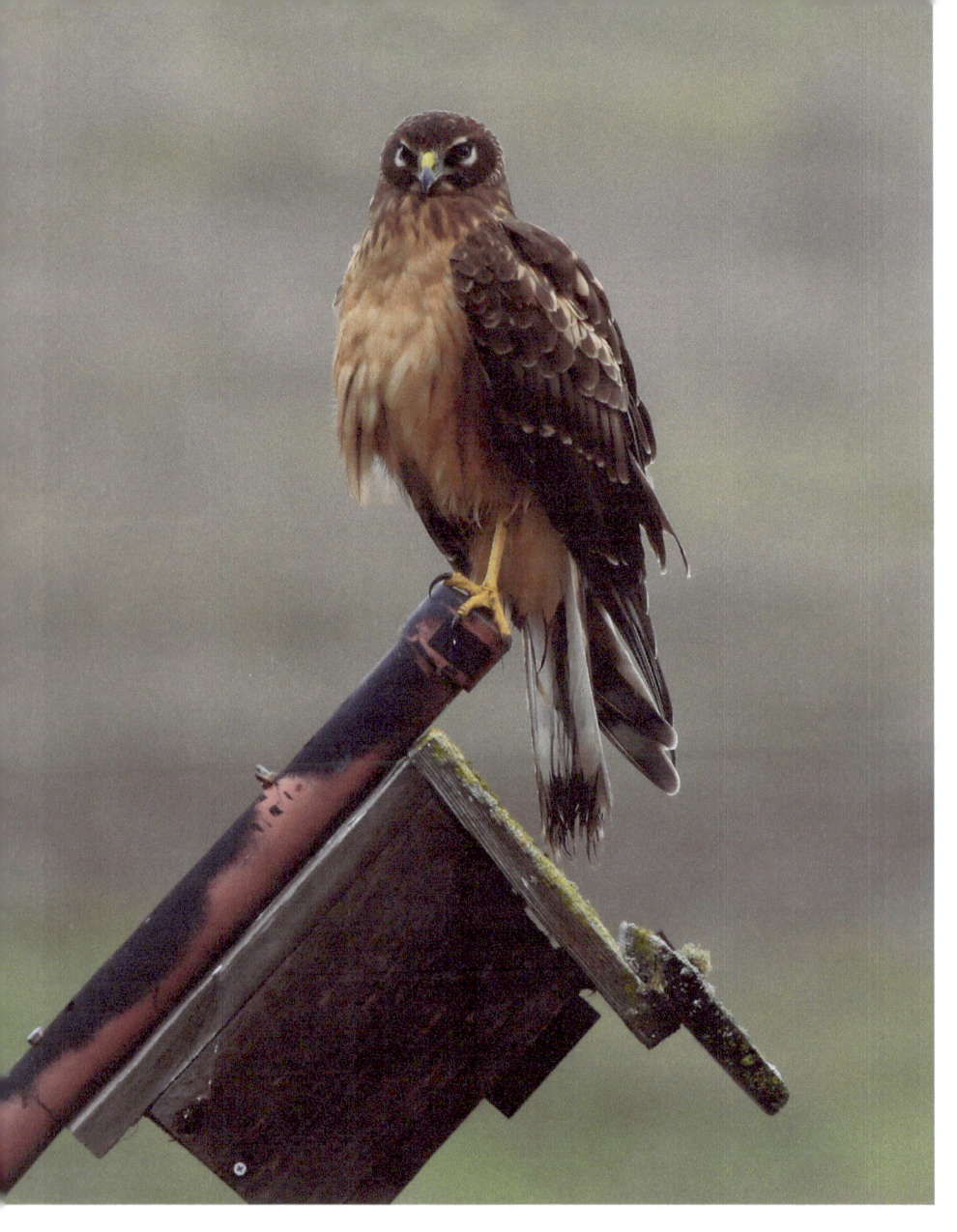

Marsh Harrier

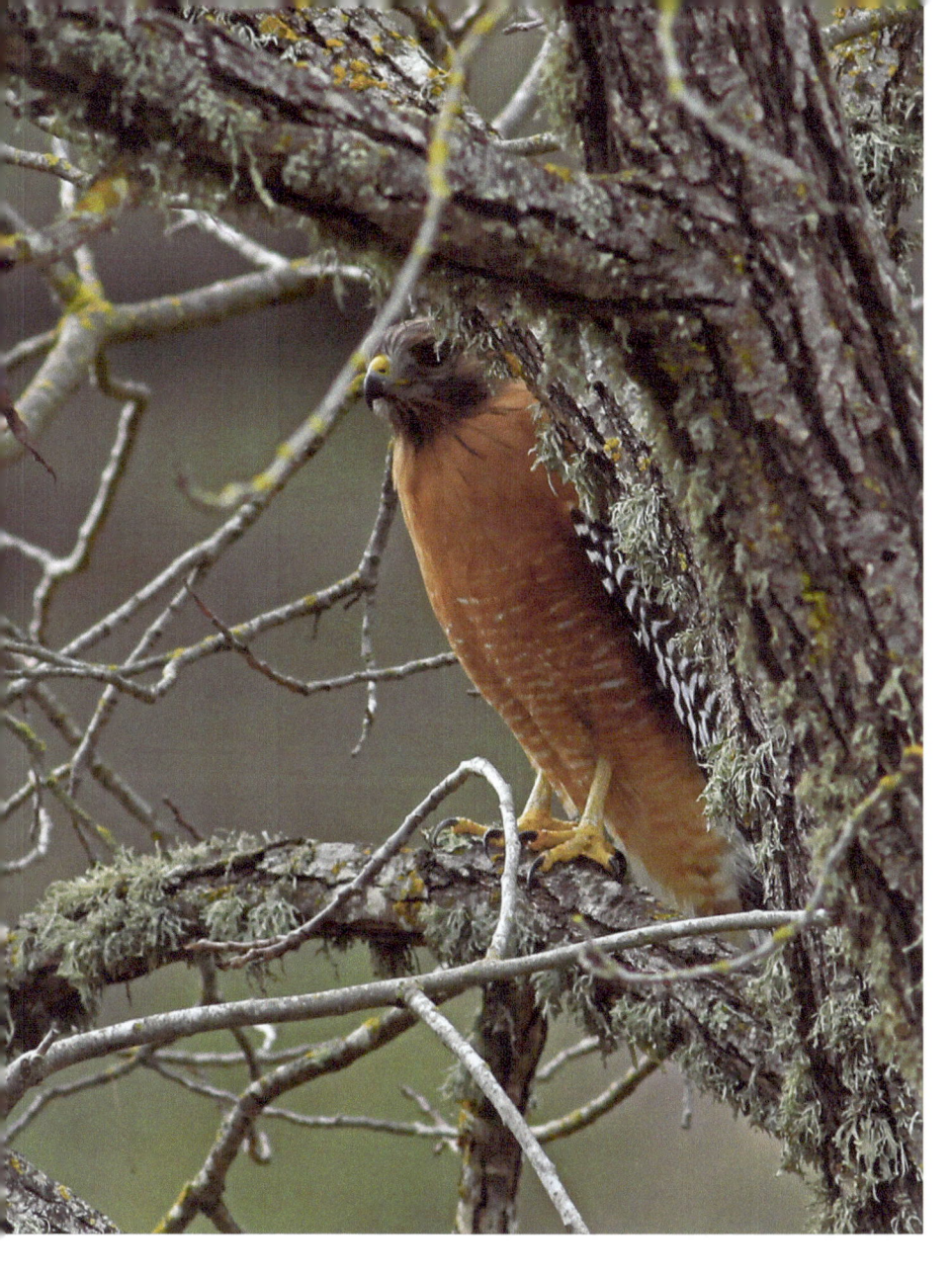

Red-shouldered Hawk

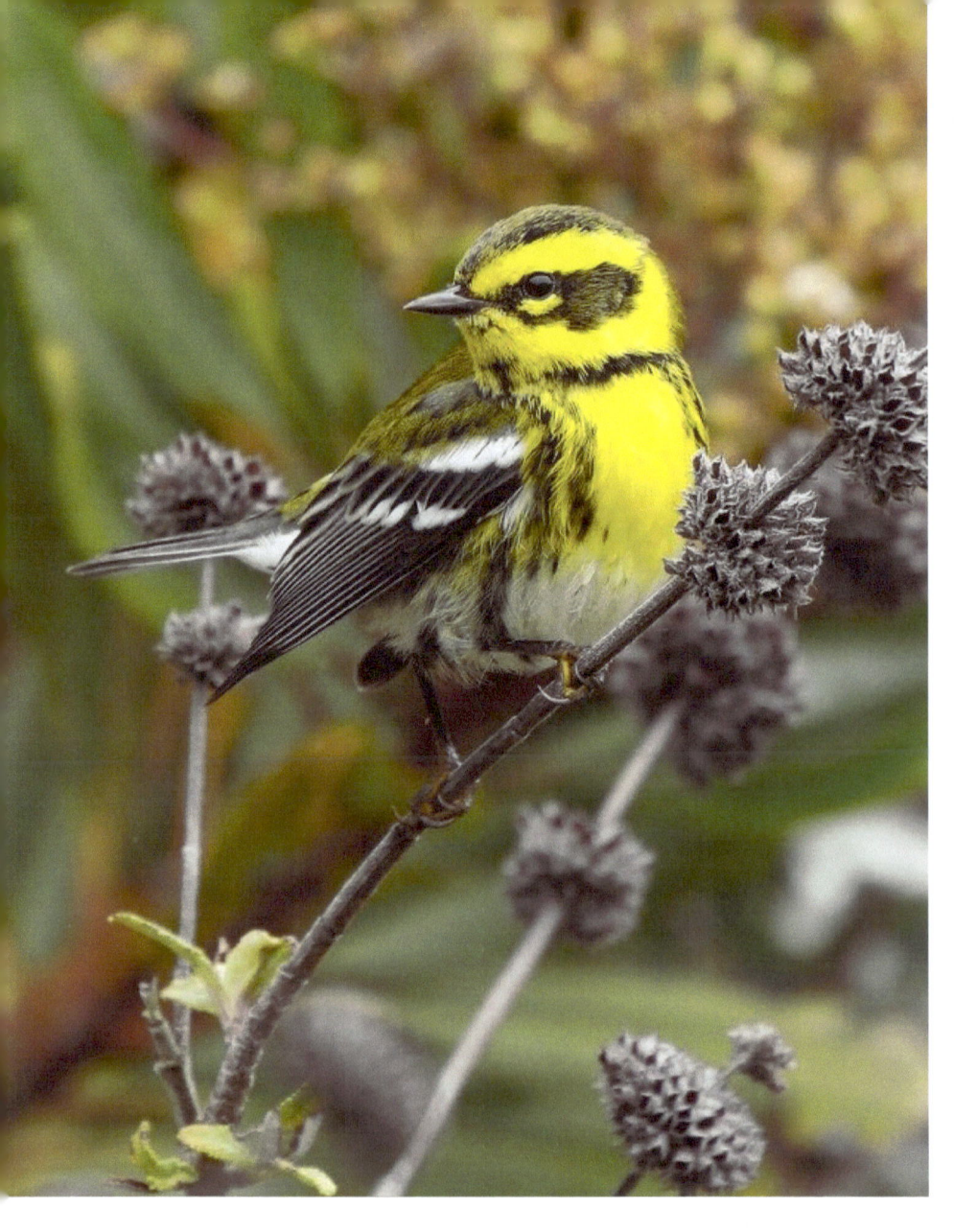

Townsend's Warbler

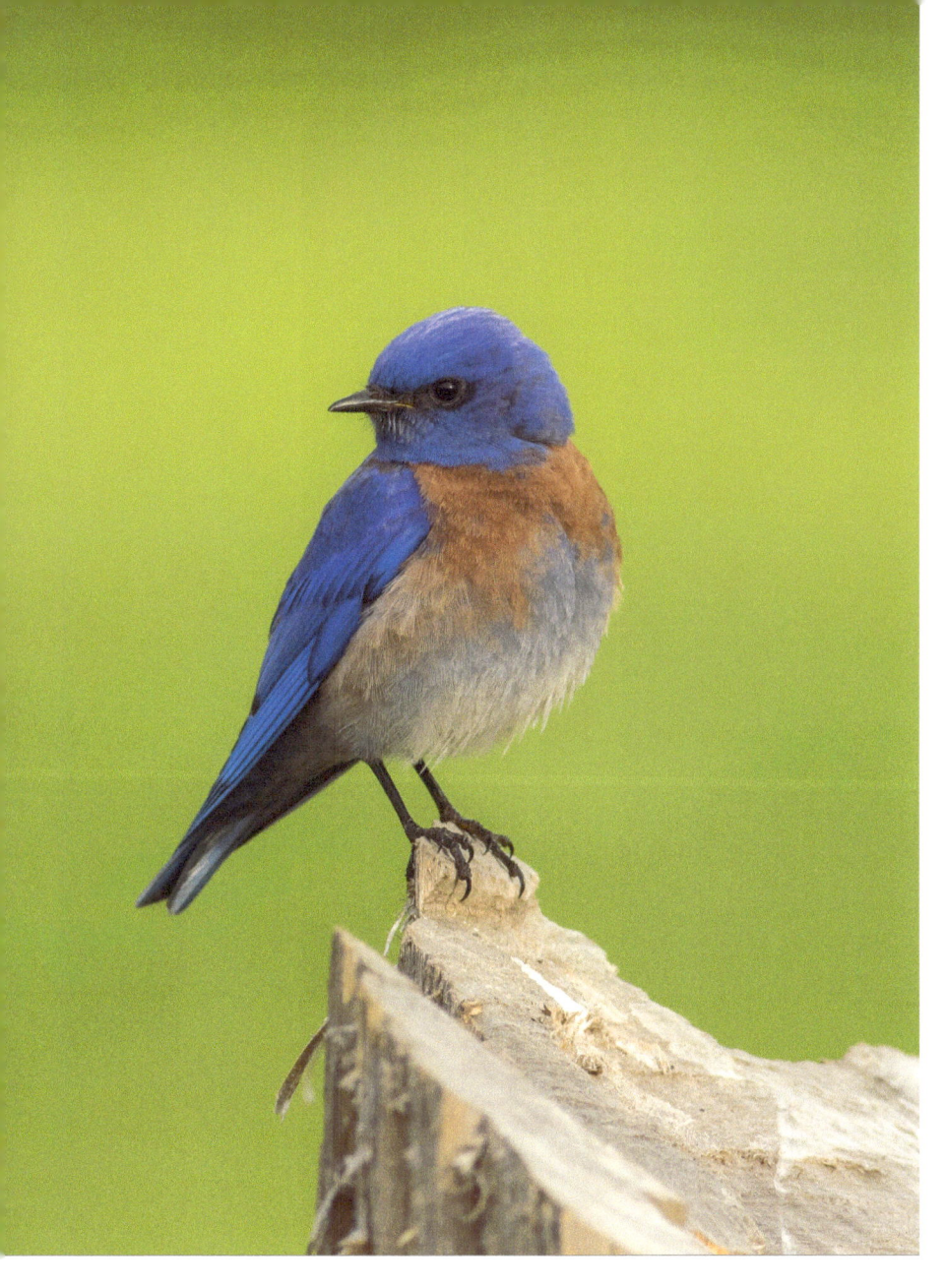

Western Bluebird

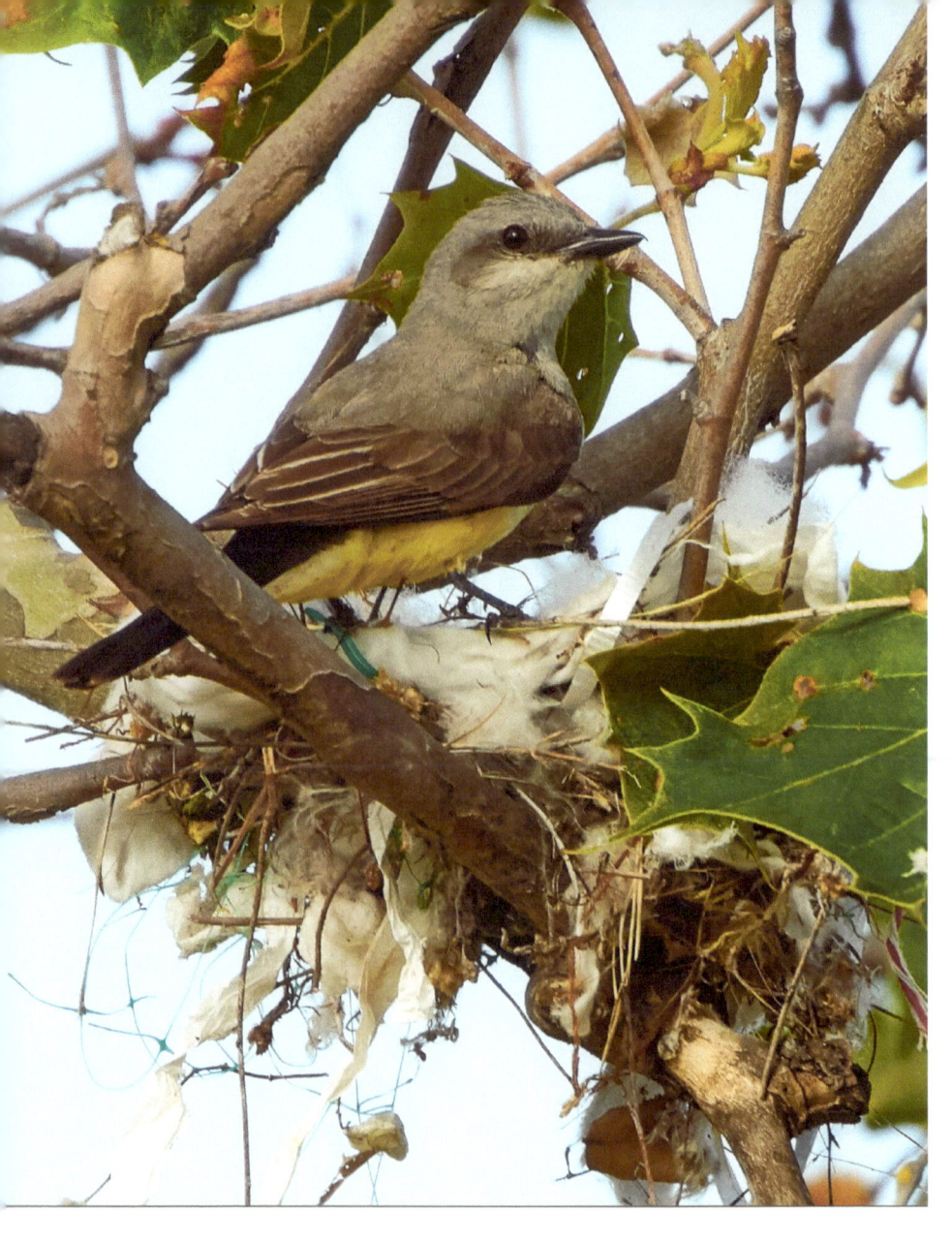

Western Kingbird

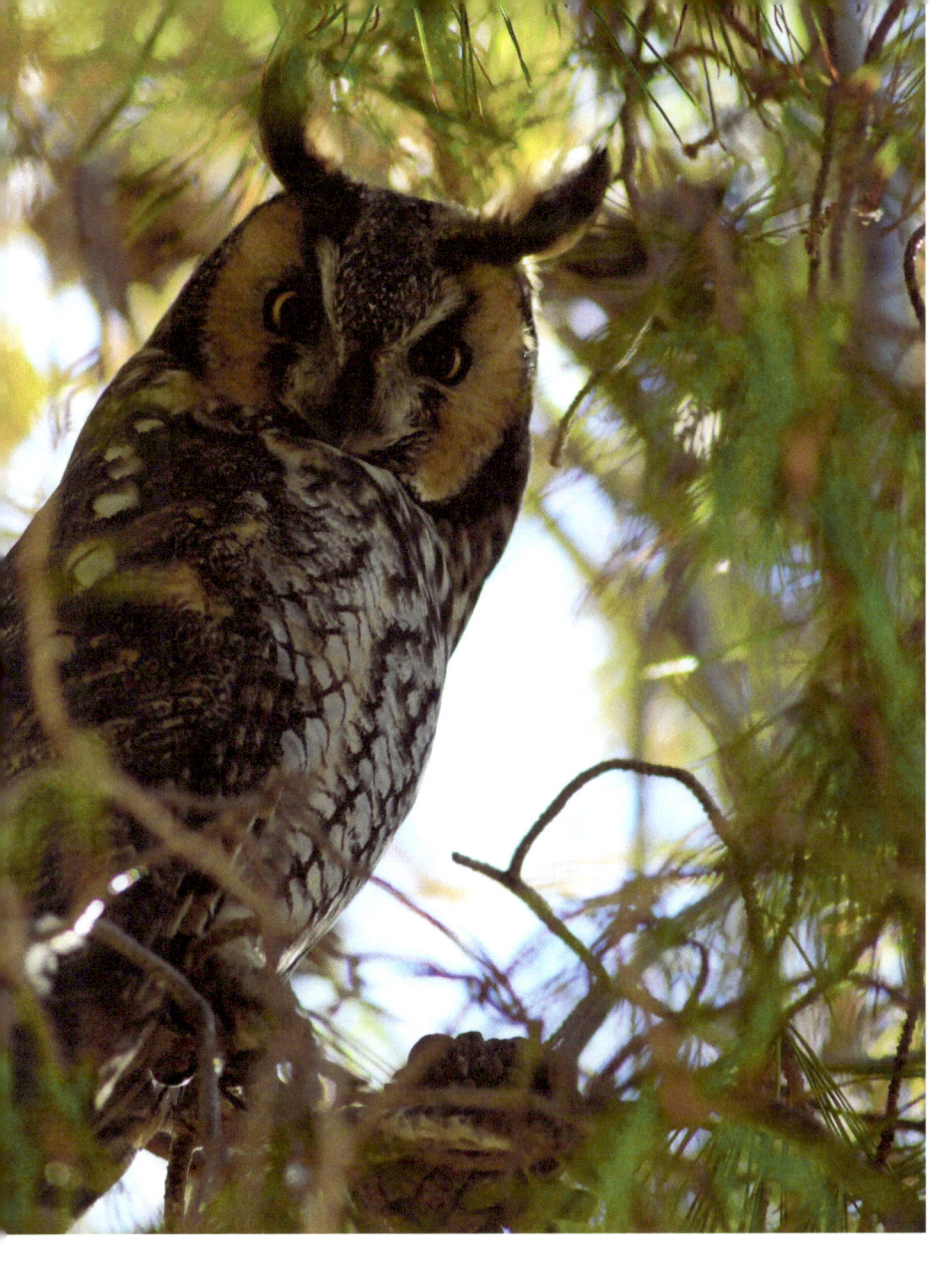

Long-eared Owl

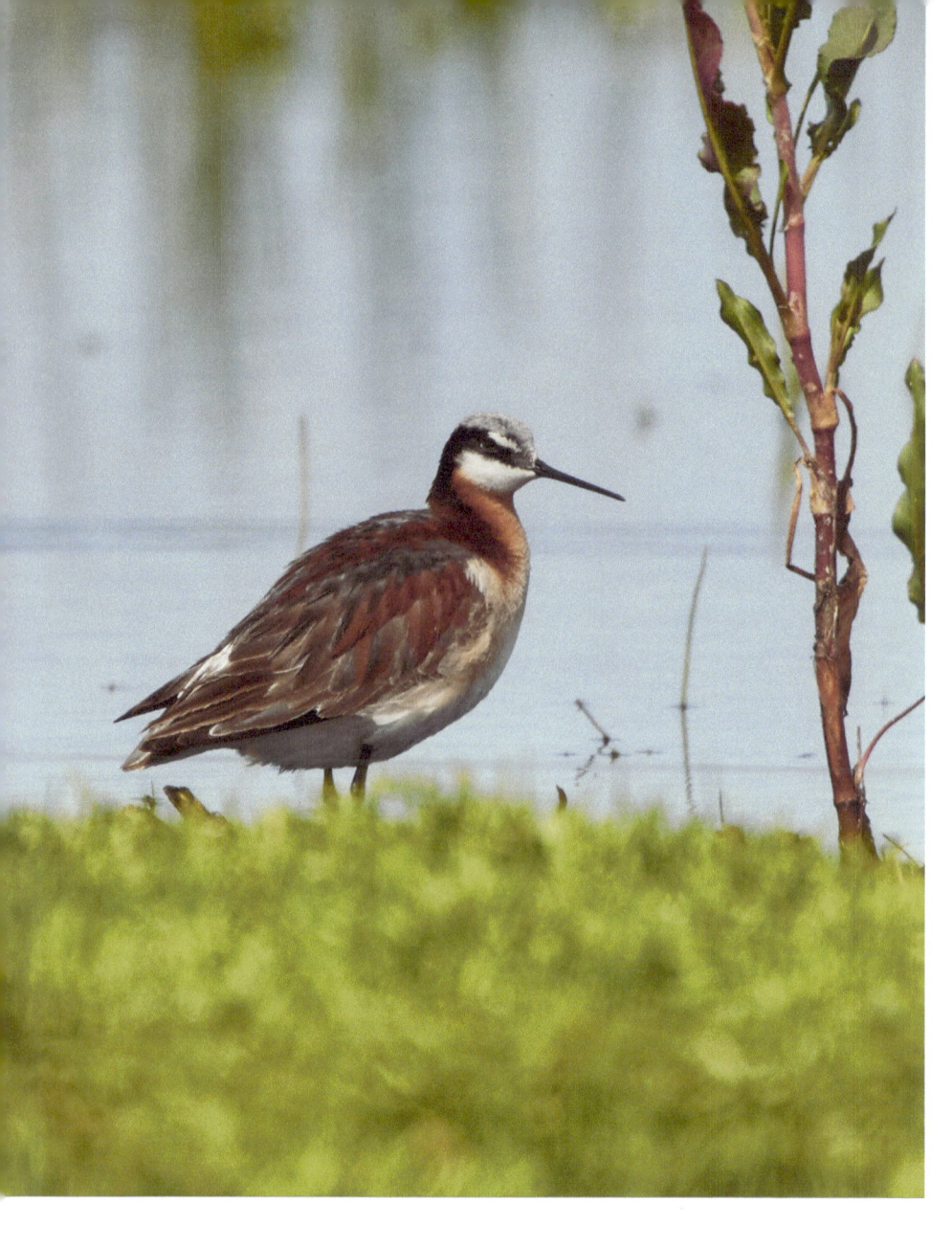

Wilson's Phalarope

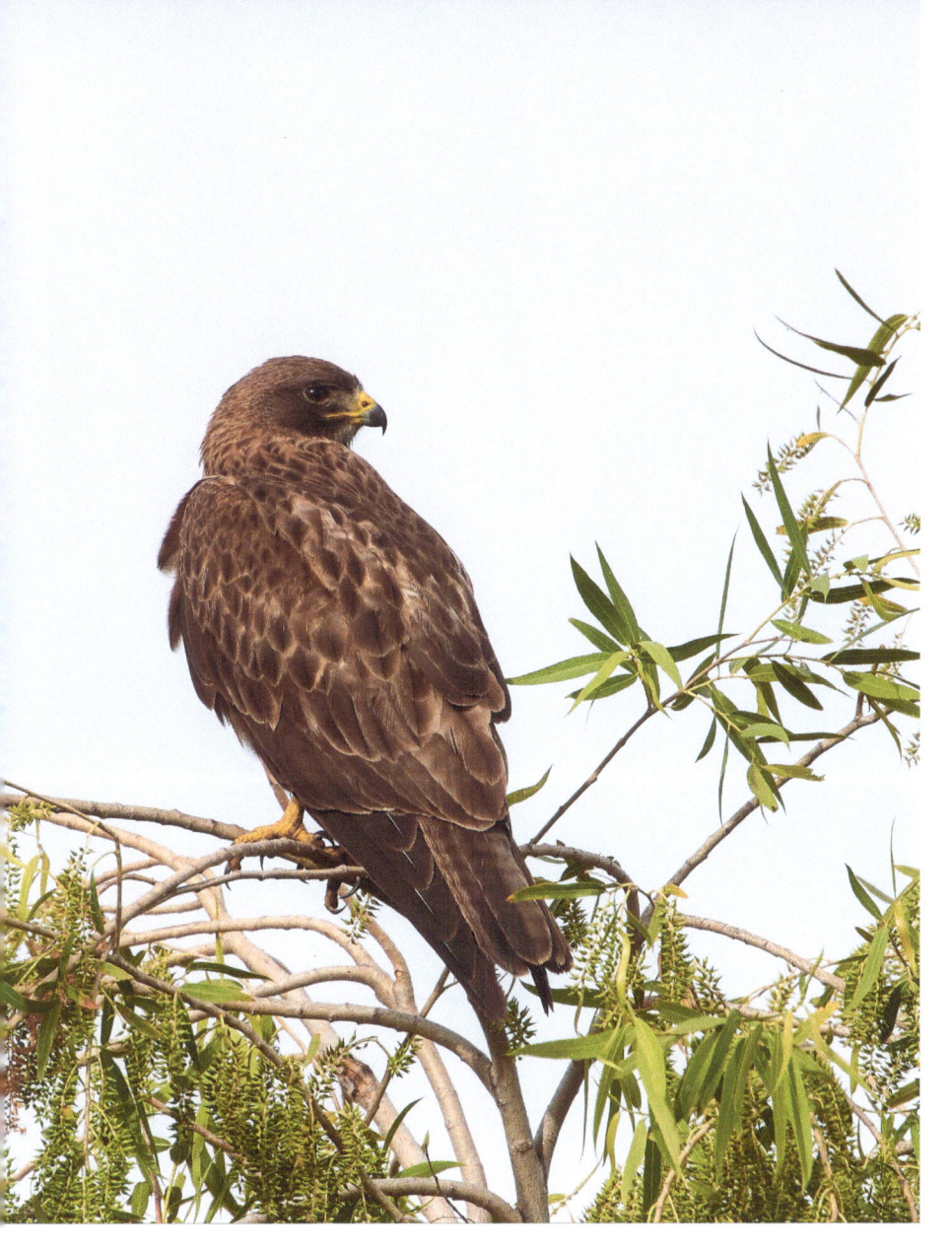

Swainson's Hawk

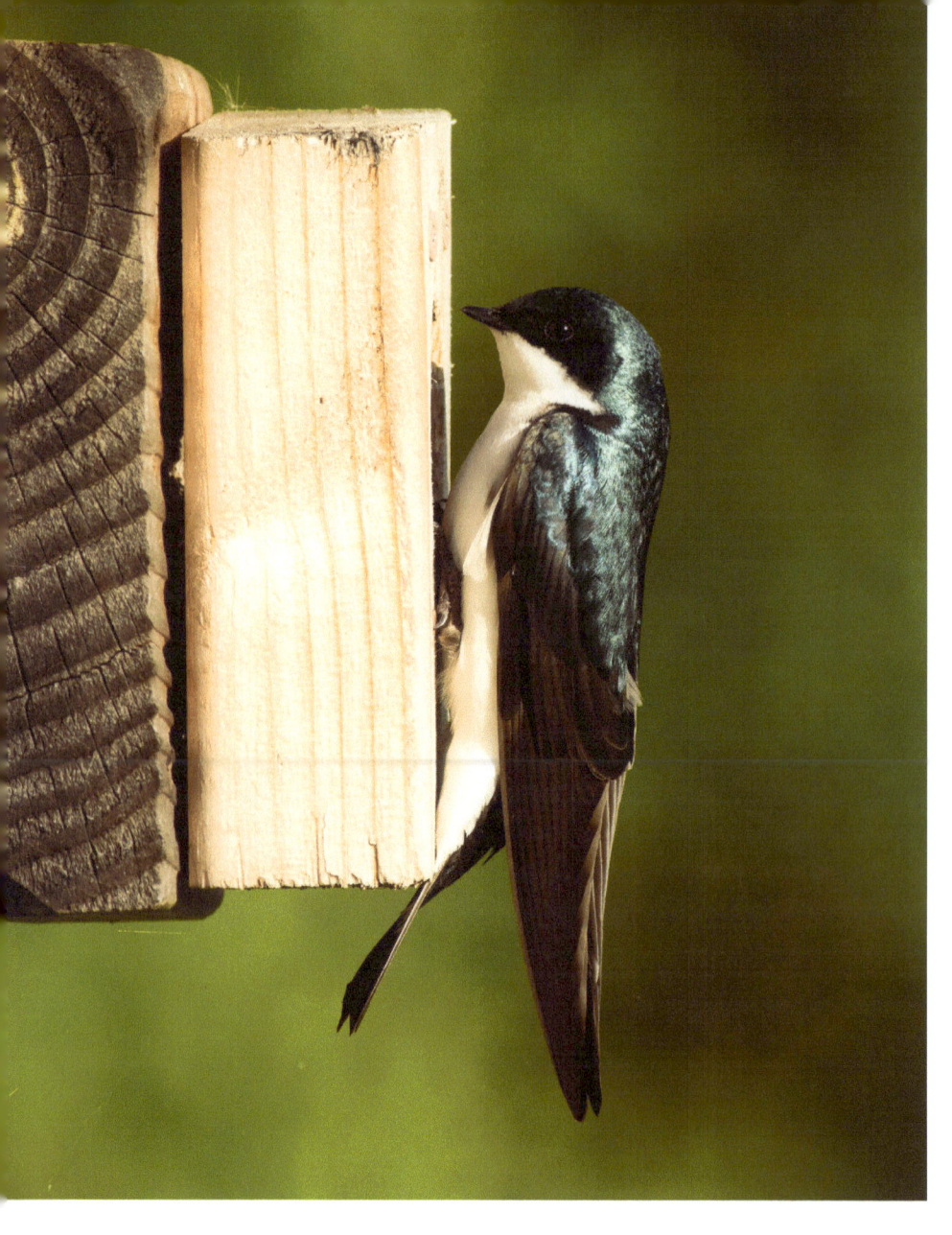

Tree Swallow

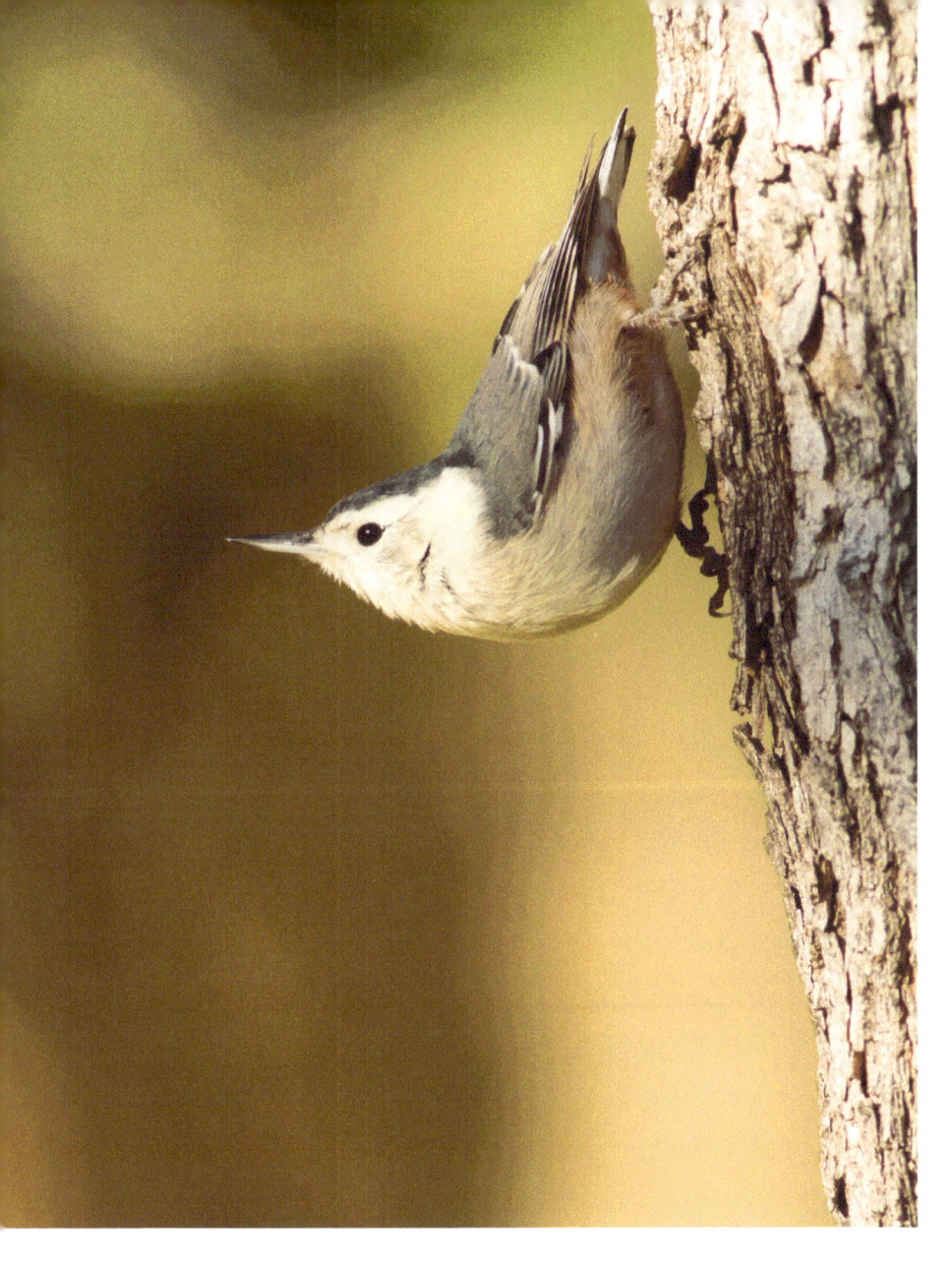

White-breasted Nuthatch

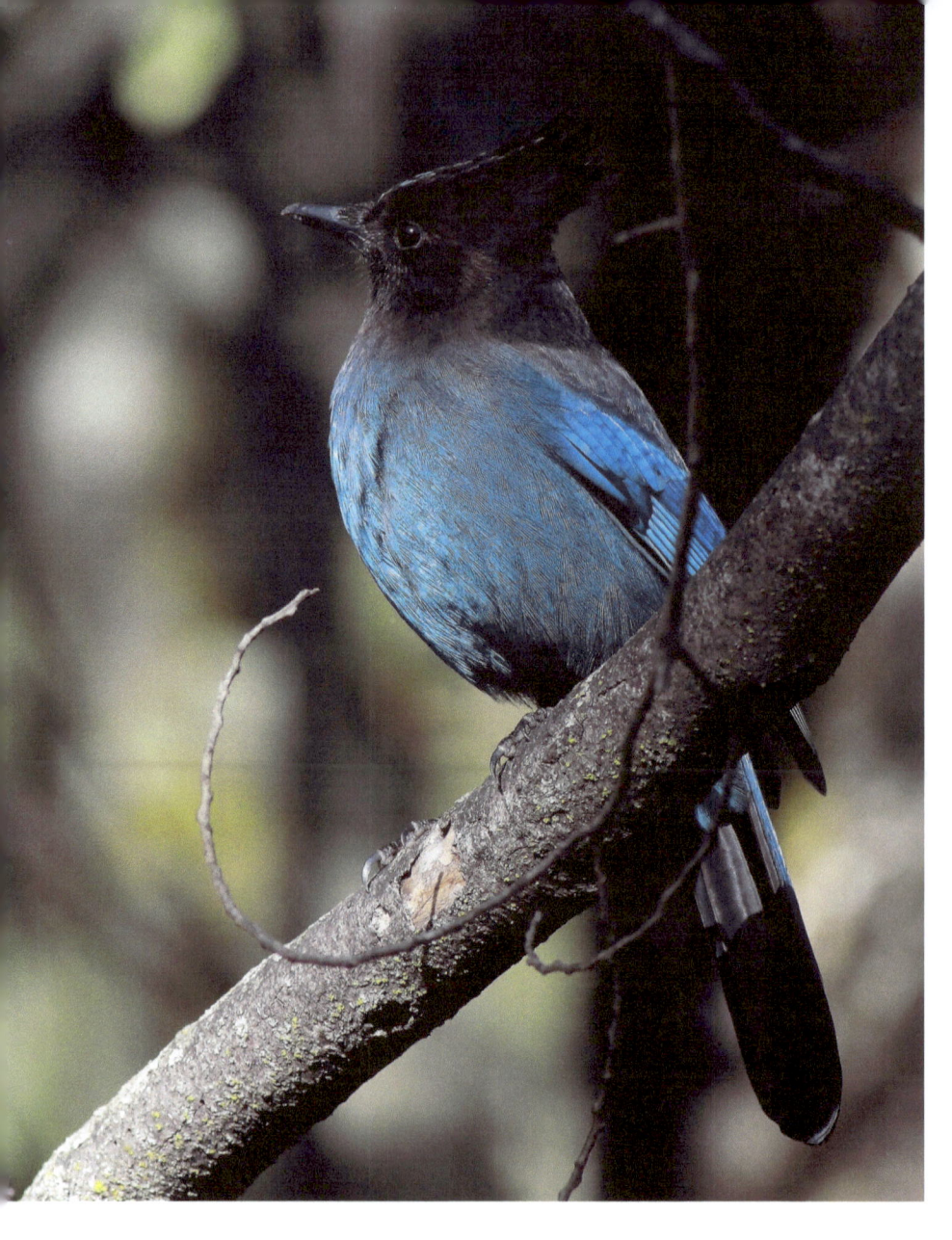

Steller's Jay

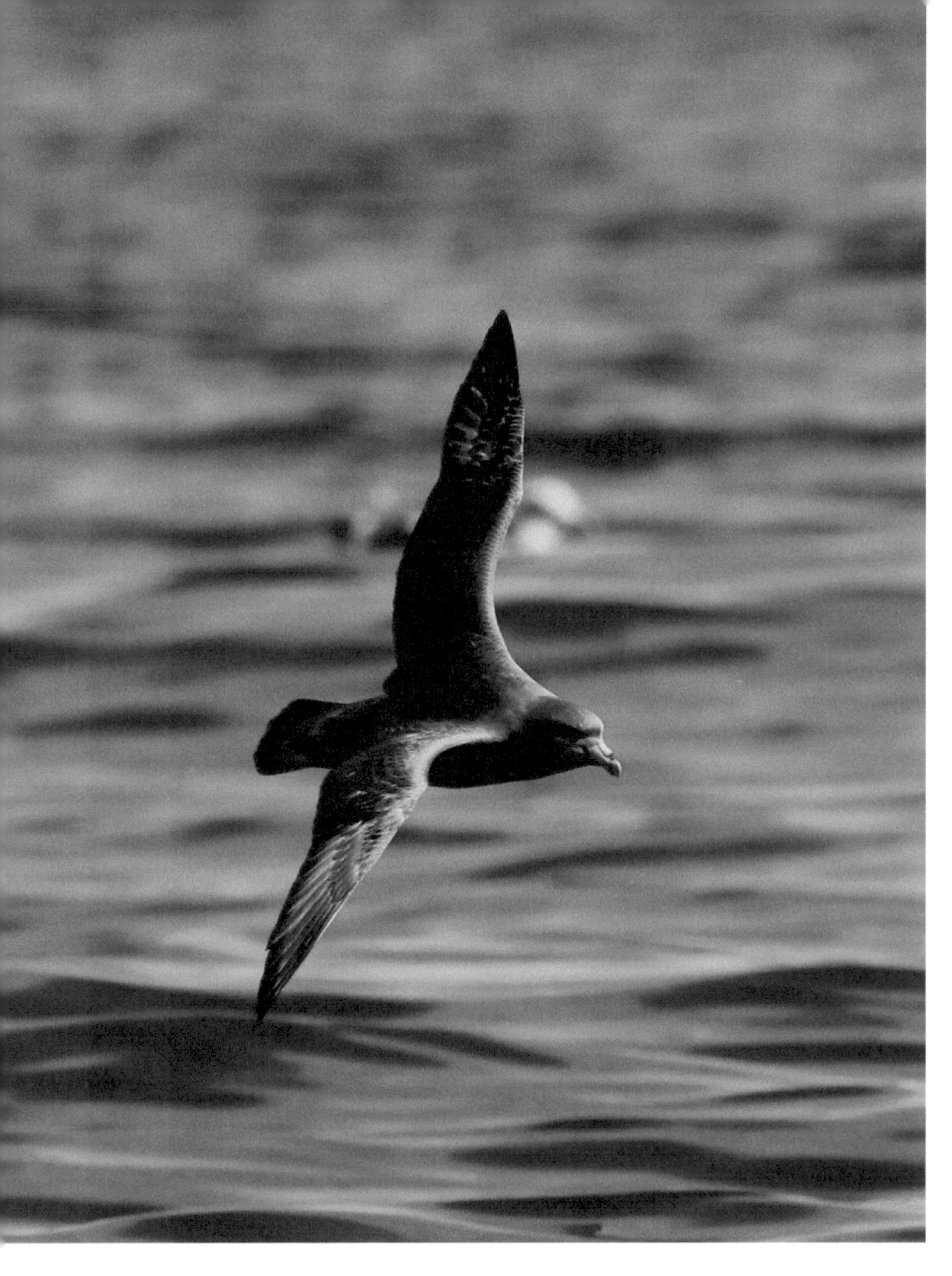

Northern Fulmar

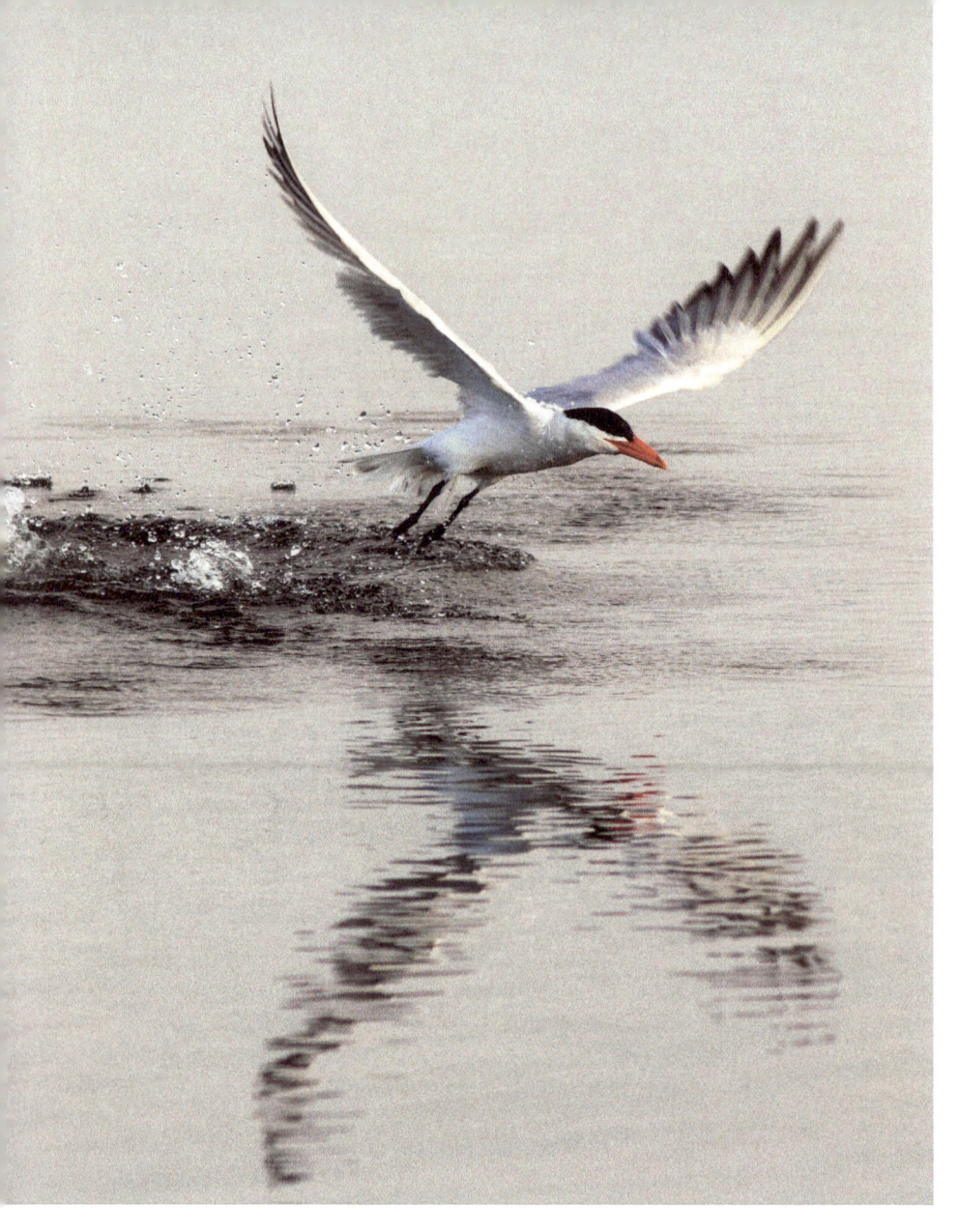

Caspian Tern

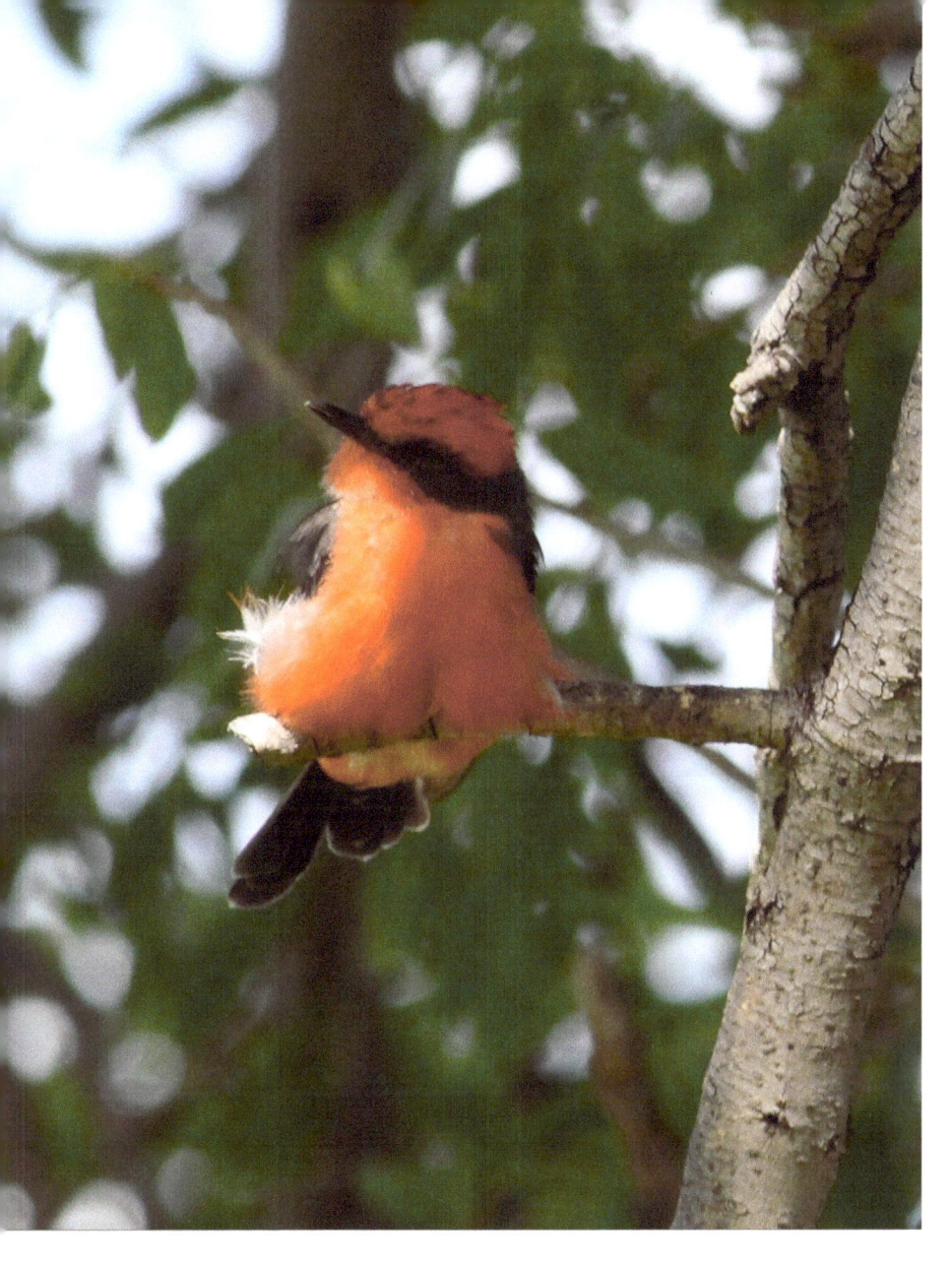

Vermillion Flycatcher

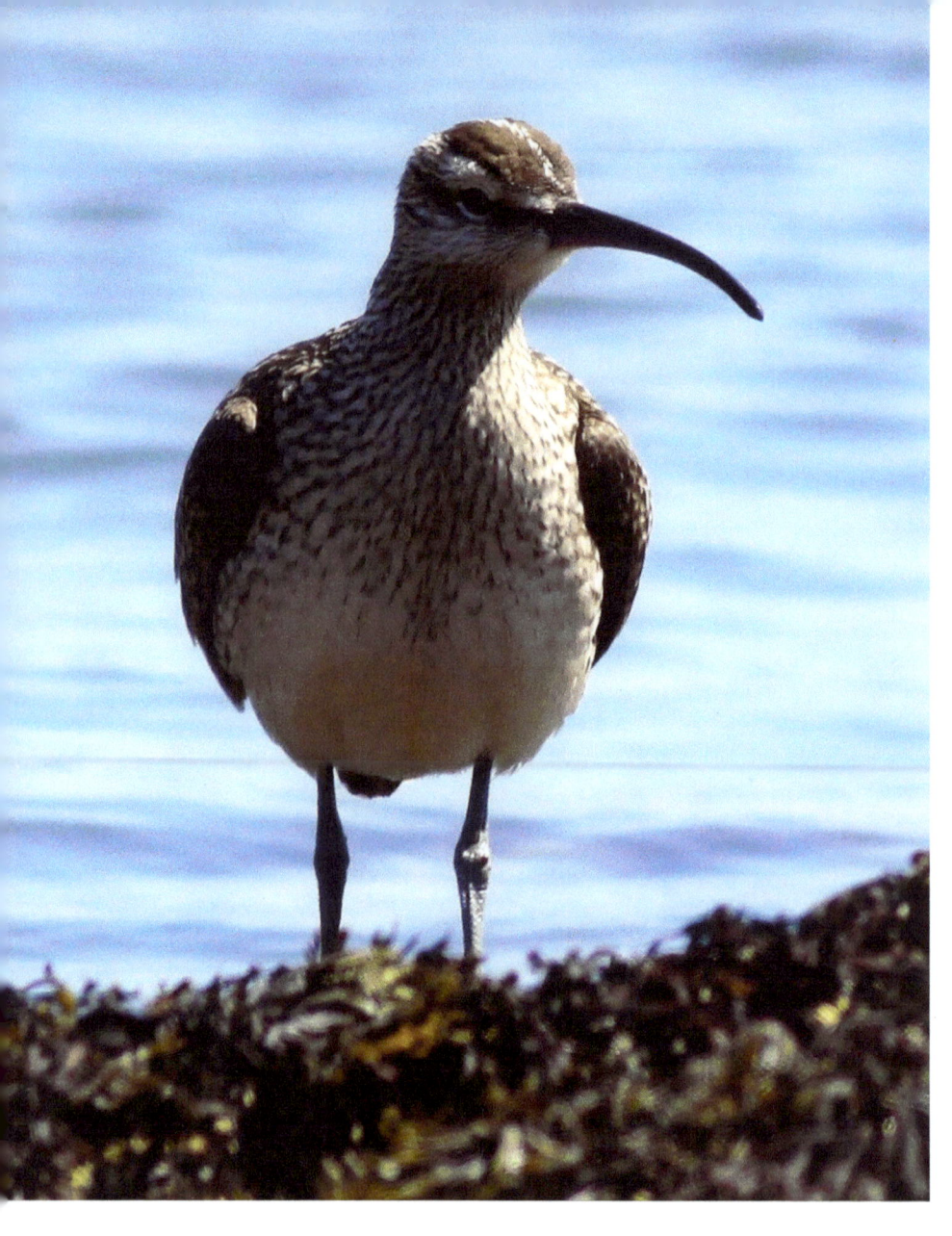

Whimbrel

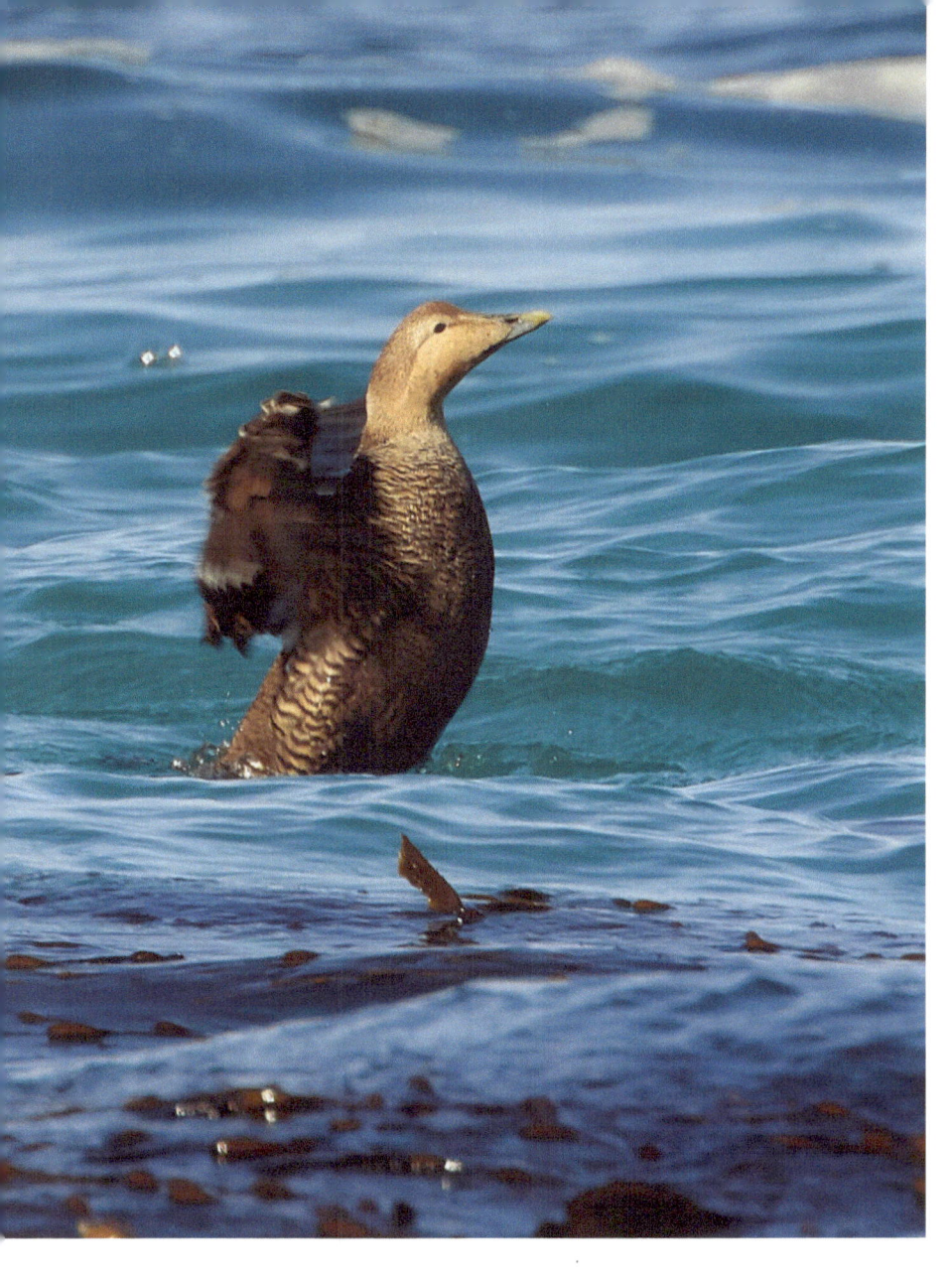

Common Eider

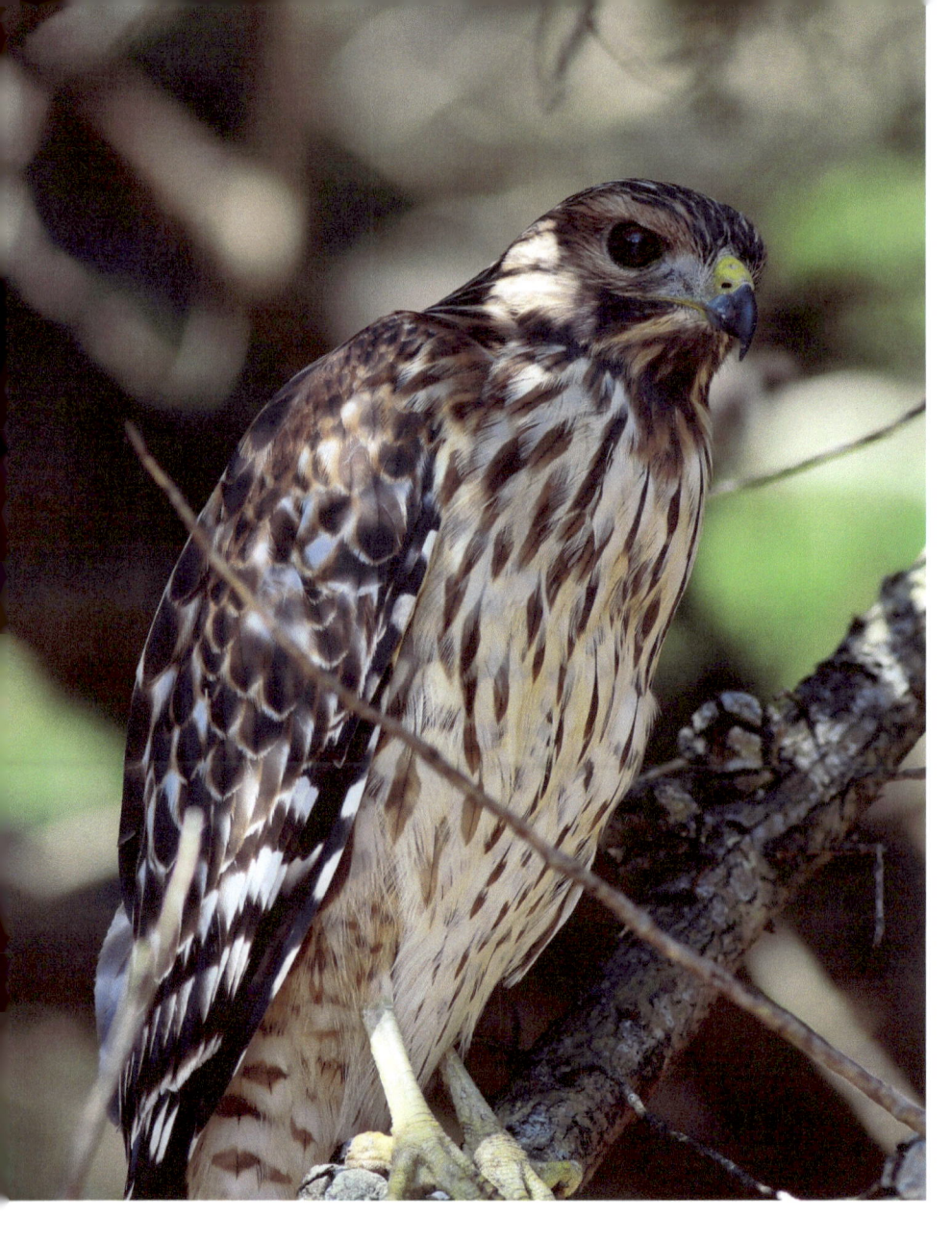

Red-shouldered Hawk

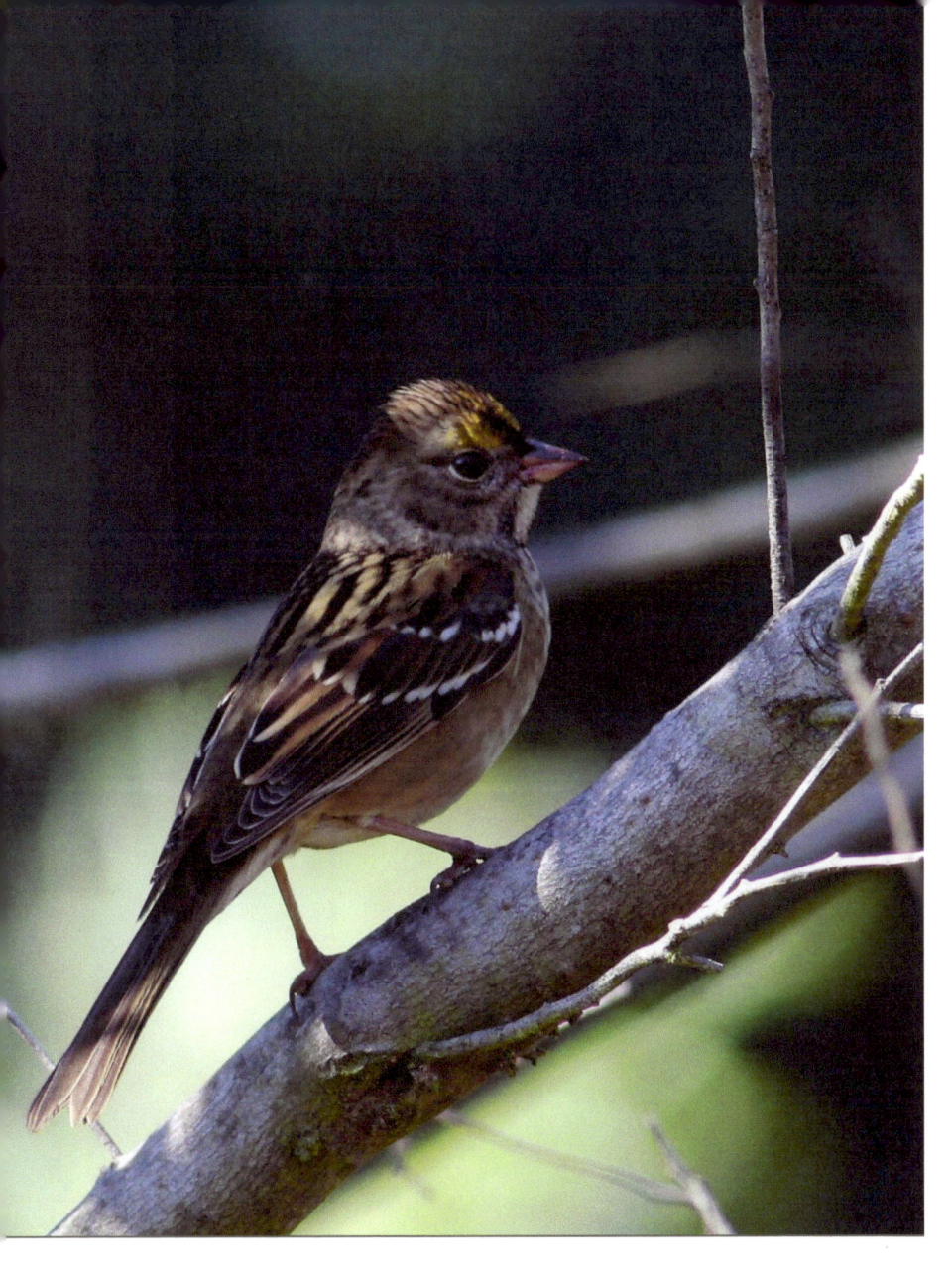

Golden Crowned Sparrow

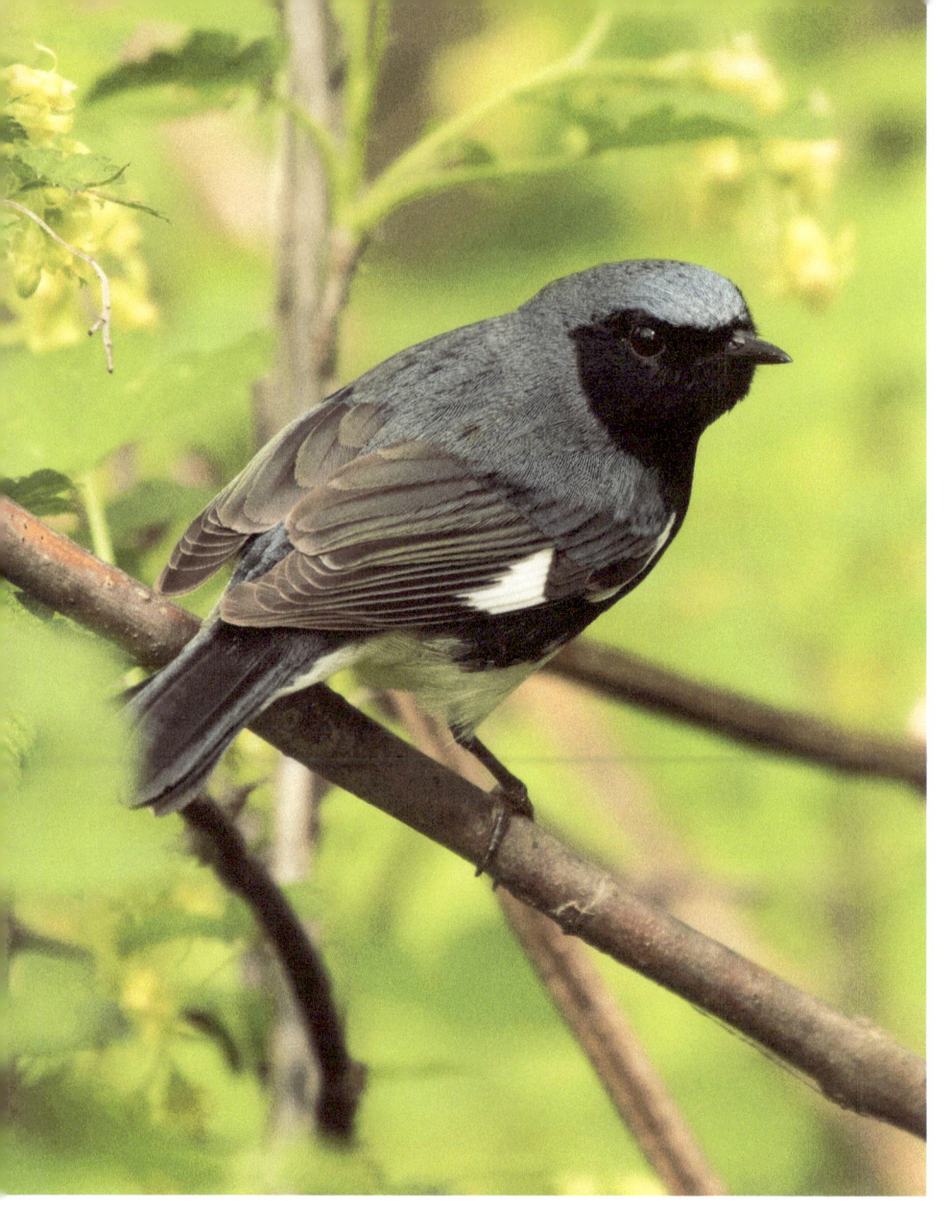

Black-throated Blue Warbler

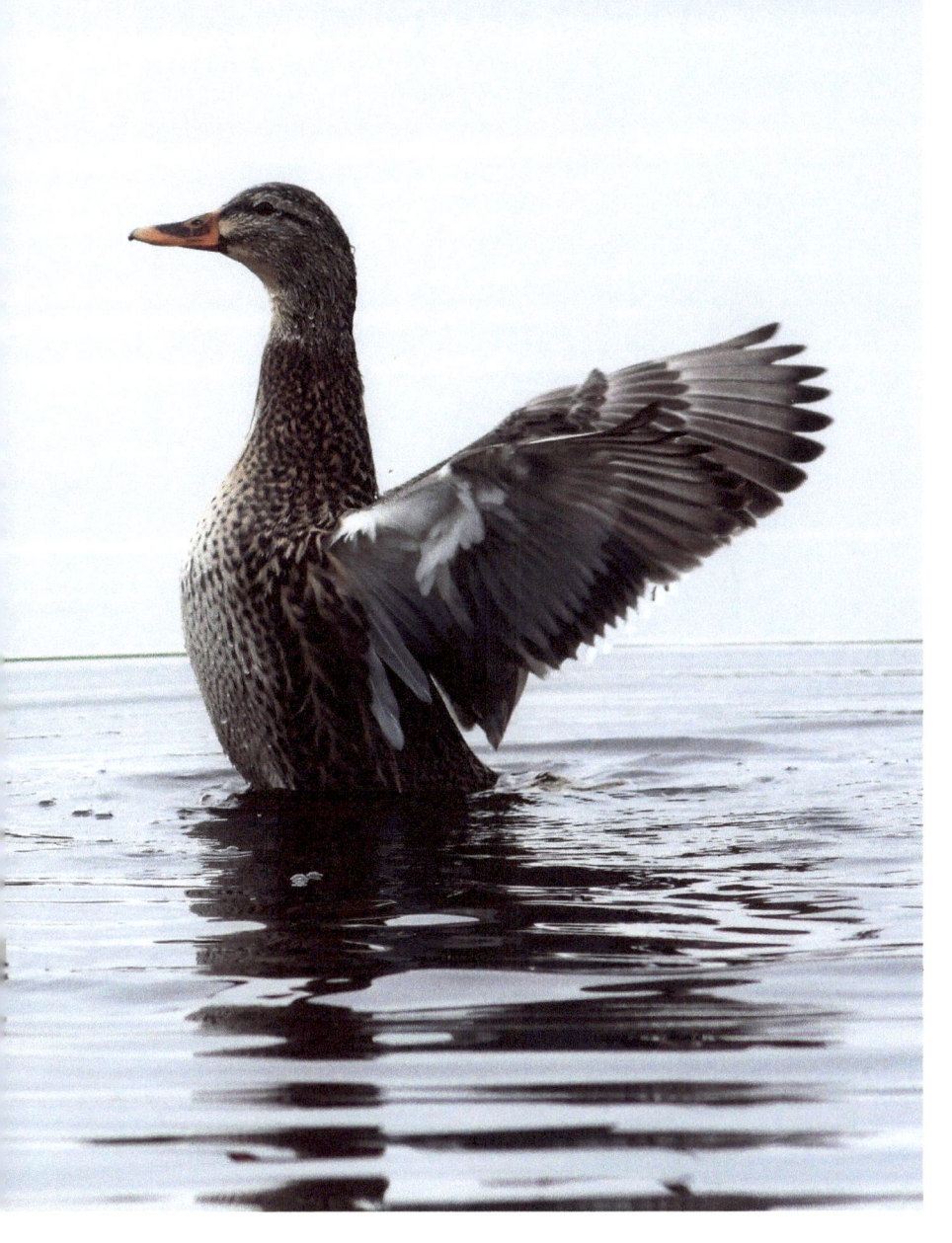

Mallard Duck

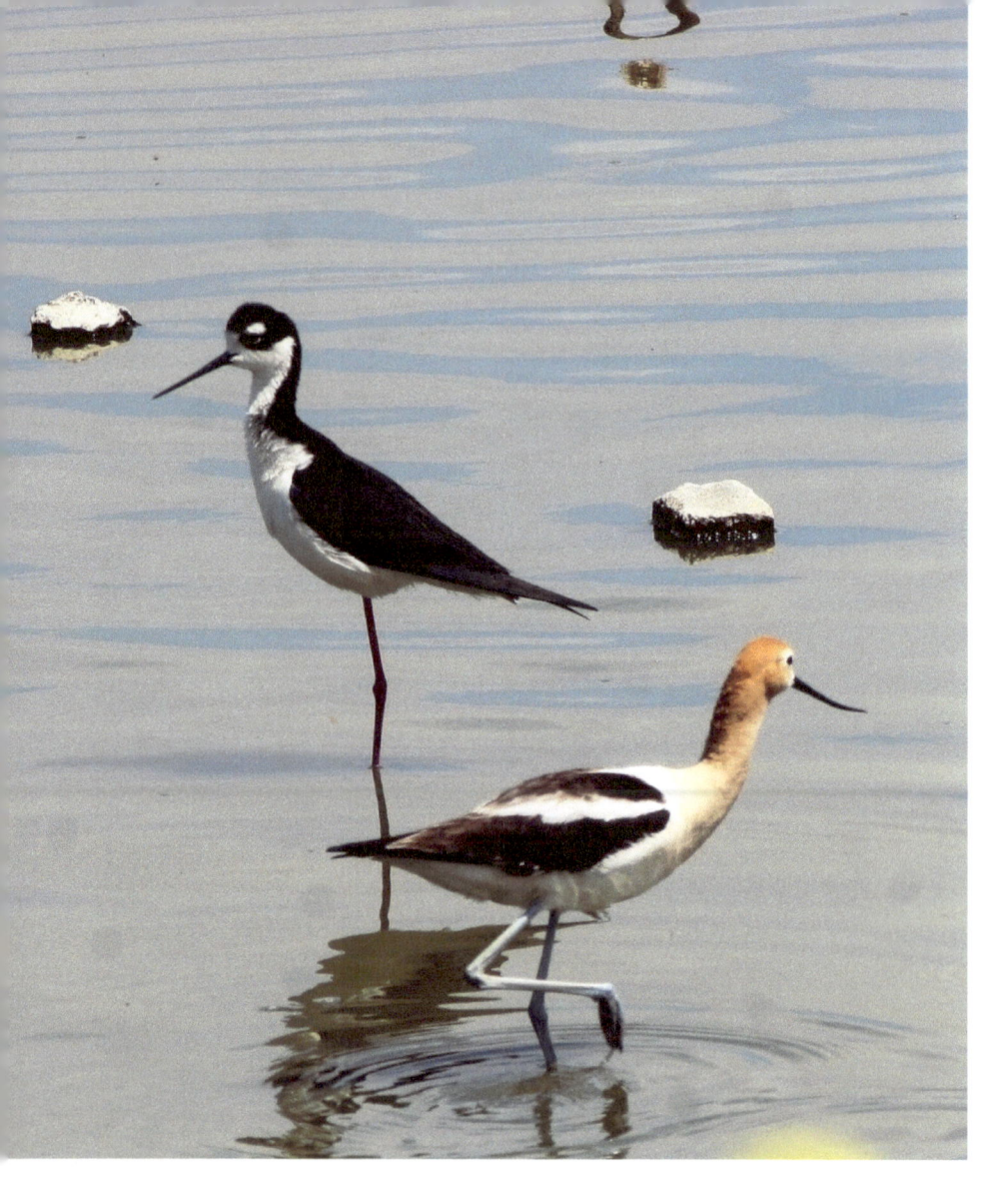

Black-necked Stilt
and American Avocet

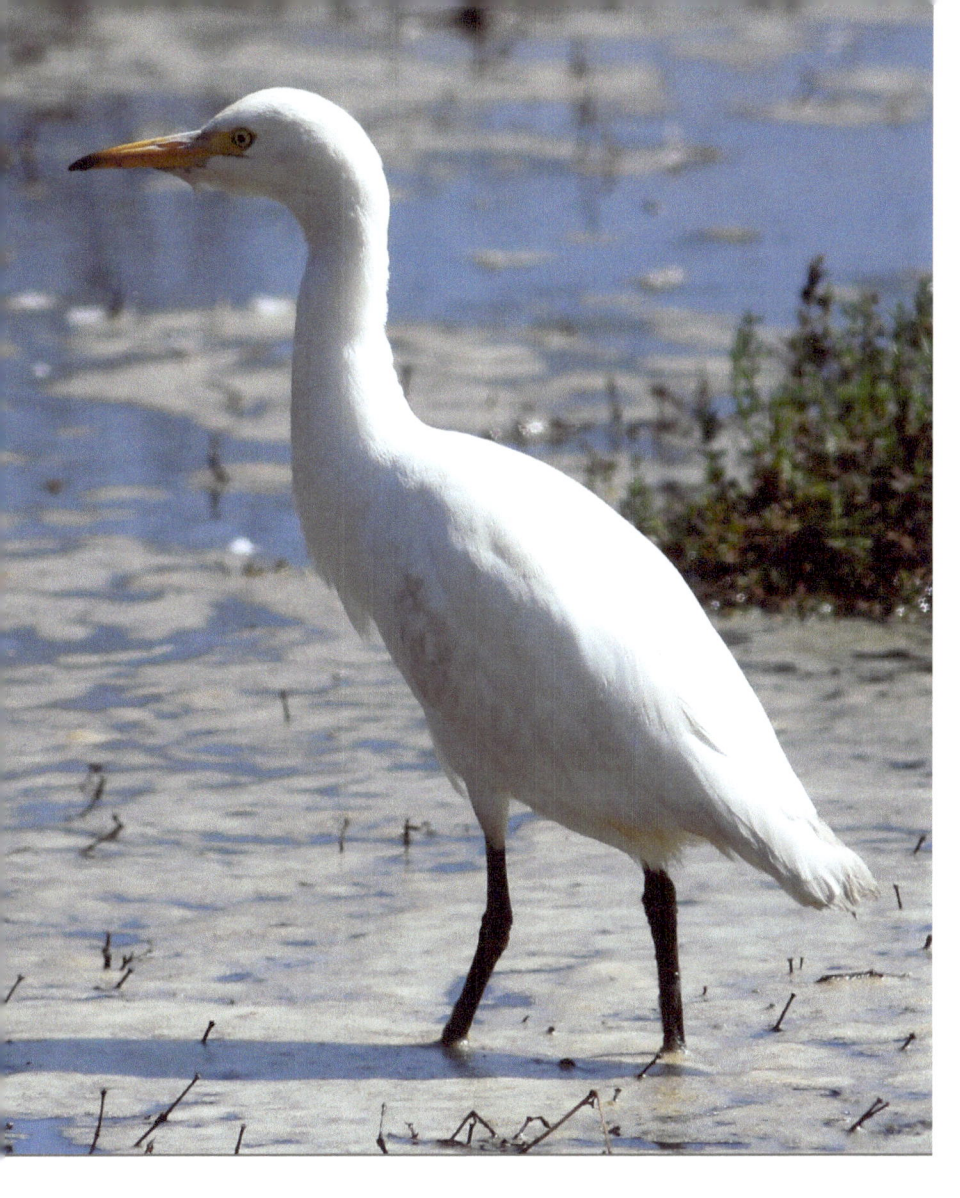

Cattle Egret

www.ingramcontent.com/pod-product-compliance
Lightning Source LLC
Chambersburg PA
CBHW041108180526

45172CB00001B/167